IRONMAN'S

Ultimate Guide to Bodybuilding Nutrition

IRONMAN'S

ULTIMATE GUIDE TO BODYBUILDING NUTRITION

IRONMAN MAGAZINE **AND PETER SISCO**

CB
CONTEMPORARY BOOKS

Library of Congress Cataloging-in-Publication Data

Ironman's ultimate guide to bodybuilding nutrition / Ironman magazine
  and Peter Sisco [editor].
        p.   cm. — (Ironman series; bk.3)
      ISBN 0-8092-2812-2
      1. Athletes—Nutrition.   2. Bodybuilding.   I. Sisco, Peter.
II. Ironman.   III. Series.
   TX361.A8I76   2000
   613.2'024'796—dc21
                                                99-39471
                                                   CIP

Cover design by Todd Petersen
Cover photograph copyright © Michael Neveux. All rights reserved.
Cover model: B. J. Quinn
Interior design by Hespenheide Design

Published by Contemporary Books
A division of NTC/Contemporary Publishing Group, Inc.
4255 West Touhy Avenue, Lincolnwood (Chicago), Illinois 60712-1975 U.S.A.
Printed in the United States of America
International Standard Book Number: 0-8092-2812-2

00 01 02 03 04 05 VL 19 18 17 16 15 14 13 12 11 10 9 8 7 6 5 4 3 2 1

CONTENTS

FOREWORD

Ironman magazine was founded in 1936 by Peary and Mabel Rader of Alliance, Nebraska. Their first print run of 50 copies was done via a duplicating machine that sat on their dining room table. *Ironman* started out as an educational vehicle to inform and enlighten those people who were interested in weight lifting, bodybuilding, and, eventually, powerlifting.

The focus of *Ironman* magazine during its first 50 years was on all three sports, with emphasis on weight training in general as a life-enhancing activity. *Ironman* has always stressed the health and character-building aspects of weight training and has always been the leader in bringing exercise and nutrition concepts and ideas to those in the training world.

In the early '50s, *Ironman* magazine was the first weight-training publication to show women working out with weights as part of their overall fitness regimen. It even went so far as to show a pregnant woman training with weights and educating readers on the benefits of exercise during pregnancy—thoroughly modern concepts 25 years ahead of its time. In the late '50s and early '60s, *Ironman* magazine was the first to talk about high-quality proteins derived from milk and eggs as well as liquid amino acids. The bimonthly magazine had, by this time, acquired over 30,000 subscribers simply on the strength of its information. The Raders never worked at expanding its circulation. It grew by word of mouth fueled by the general hunger for and *Ironman*'s ability to provide intelligent, timely, and reliable training information.

By the early '80s, the Raders, now in their 70s, had spent nearly 50 years working incredibly long hours to put out a bimonthly publication. The hard work was beginning to take its toll.

I'd been interested in *Ironman* as a business since the mid-'70s and had in fact talked several times with the Raders about purchasing *Ironman*. Eventually, my dream of owning and publishing a bodybuilding magazine was realized, and in August 1986, after 50 years, *Ironman* magazine changed owners. At that time, *Ironman* had a circulation of 30,000 subscribers, had no foreign editions, was published bimonthly, and averaged 96 black-and-white pages, with a color cover. Thirteen years later, *Ironman* magazine is published worldwide with an English-language circulation of 225,000 and additional editions in Japanese, Italian, German, Arabic, and Russian.

The books in the *Ironman* series represent the "best of the best" articles from over 60 years of *Ironman* magazine.

John Balik
Publisher, Ironman

ACKNOWLEDGMENTS

I would like to thank the following people who made this book possible:

John Balik, publisher of *Ironman* magazine, had the foresight to see the need for this book and the others in the *Ironman* series. His knowledge of bodybuilding and his sensitivity to the information required by readers has made *Ironman* the best bodybuilding magazine in the world.

Steve Holman, editor in chief of *Ironman*, creates one informative, insightful issue of the magazine after another, and his own article in this book shows ample evidence of his innovation and encyclopedic knowledge of the iron game.

Mike Neveux is the premier bodybuilding photographer in the world. His photos in this book and in every issue of *Ironman* magazine have inspired and motivated countless bodybuilders around the world by capturing the intensity, power, and magnificence of these great athletes.

A special thanks to Terry Bratcher, art director of *Ironman*, who did an enormous amount of work in the preparation of this book by wading through *Ironman*'s immense archive of articles and photographs in order to help bring you the "best of the best."

Finally, I would like to thank all the writers who contributed to this book. These writers have an incalculable collective knowledge of the sport of bodybuilding. This book represents the distilled knowledge of hundreds of man-years of study in every aspect and nuance of the iron game. Between the covers of this book are wisdom and experience that would cost a small fortune to obtain from one-on-one training with these writers. Sadly, some are no longer with us to be able to share their vast insights, making their advice in these pages all the more valuable. It is the thought, effort, and writing of these individuals that make this book and *Ironman* magazine great.

Peter Sisco
Editor

INTRODUCTION

Peary Rader, through the pages of *Ironman* in the 1950s, was the first person to bring the concept of six or more "feedings" per day to bodybuilding. He saw it as the optimal way of increasing muscle mass while storing the least amount of fat. He made that observation based on the collection of anecdotal evidence he had gathered in his many conversations with successful bodybuilders. As the concept spread, it became apparent that it was a far superior way of eating than the "three square meals" idea that is so ingrained in our culture.

At around the same time Irvin Johnson, who later changed his name to Rheo Blair, added the thought that at least three of the minimeals could and should be a liquid concentrated source of protein. Blair, in fact, started a bodybuilding revolution with the help of Peary Rader.

Today *Ironman* continues to lead the way in nutrition thanks to a number of researchers and authorities, including Daniel Gwartney, M.D., a well-respected medical doctor and nutrition researcher; Dan Duchaine, who is considered the guru of ergogenics; and Jerry Brainum, a renowned nutrition and training researcher and consultant to amateur and professional athletes. In each issue of *Ironman* these authors, along with numerous others, explore nutrition and supplementation and help readers demystify diet. You'll find examples of that in this book as well.

John Balik
Publisher, Ironman

IRONMAN'S

ULTIMATE GUIDE TO
BODYBUILDING
NUTRITION

Skip La Cour.

Chapter 1

MASS MACHINE SUPPLEMENTATION
STRATEGIES FOR BUILDING A CHAMPIONSHIP PHYSIQUE

BY SKIP LA COUR

Recent advances in nutritional supplementation have been helping natural bodybuilders develop especially impressive physiques these days. The scientific research behind supplementation is progressing at an incredible rate, and, if you're a bodybuilder who's committed to becoming the best you can be, you'd be foolish not to take advantage of it.

Does that mean you should go to your local health-food store and stock up on the many pills, capsules, powders, and liquids available? Certainly not! To be a smart and successful consumer you must first invest some time in understanding the proper role of supplements in your overall bodybuilding efforts and then create an intelligent and organized plan based on the latest information available.

THE PROPER ROLE OF SUPPLEMENTS

"For top performance, food is first," insists Dr. Michael Colgan.[1] I absolutely agree. When you're constructing your bodybuilding strategies, eating the right foods should be the foundation of your nutritional plan. Supplements are just what the name implies: an addition, backup support for sound nutrition and intense weight training. They aren't intended to be a magic bullet or a replacement for intelligent eating habits and good old-fashioned hard training.

Nevertheless, the modern world presents many time constraints and time challenges to time management. If you don't deal with them effectively, you can easily neutralize your bodybuilding efforts. Eating correctly—and often enough—is difficult for many people. Getting the entire array of the nutrients you need to create muscle from just the food you eat is even more difficult.

That's where good supplementation comes in. Often, it's more efficient and much easier for the body to get the nutrients it needs to build muscle with state-of-the-art meal replacements and advanced protein powders than with regular food. Moreover, these supplements can be significantly more nutritious and have only a fraction of the calories and fat.

Skip La Cour.

CREATING YOUR OWN SUPPLEMENTATION PROGRAM

The effort you put into developing your supplement program greatly influences its effectiveness, justifying its cost. Be sure to learn the specific purpose of each supplement you decide to buy. Find out what promises the manufacturer makes and what studies substantiate its claims. Ask other trainees who have used the product about their experiences.

After learning what the supplements are actually supposed to do, evaluate the priority you place on those qualities. You may be on a limited budget and unable to purchase every product available. Determine your goals, and find out which supplements will meet them and provide the best value.

The suggested effective dose and price for the supplement are also important considerations. Some supplements may be priced reasonably, but when you consider the required dosages, they're not such a great value. If they're too expensive, the odds are you can't continue using them.

Hot, or trendy, supplements come and go, so it's very important to get the most recent and reliable research available. Nothing, however, takes the place of trial and error. I developed my personal supplementation program over many years, using a lot of research and input from knowledgeable people. I added and deleted supplements only after carefully examining their impact and value.

Be sure when you add a new supplement to your program that you consider all the fac-

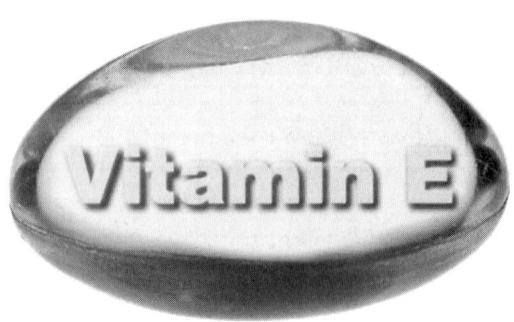

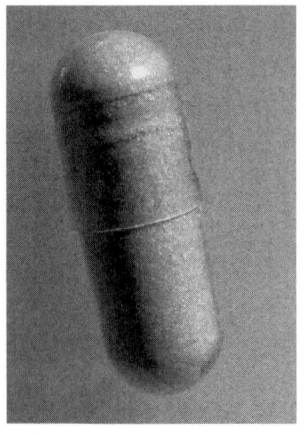

Skip La Cour.

tors that may contribute to or detract from its effectiveness. In other words, be sure you continue to train hard and eat well while experimenting with a new supplement. Always introduce one new supplement at a time so you can properly evaluate its effectiveness. It's also a good rule of thumb to introduce new supplements 30 days apart.

PROTEIN SUPPLEMENTATION

I firmly believe that a good bodybuilding supplementation program is built on a rock-solid foundation of high-quality protein supplements. The investment is well worth the cost of protein. At around 240 pounds I take in approximately 453 grams of protein a day.

About 165 grams of it, or 36 percent, come from regular food, such as chicken, tuna, and egg whites.

The other 288 grams, or a whopping 64 percent, come from high-quality whey protein in the form of convenient meal replacements. I divide the protein as evenly as possible over eight meals.

The higher the quality of the protein you put into your system, the more you'll use for muscle growth and the less you'll convert to fat. You'll better optimize your workouts and build more muscle. I would go so far as to say that 75 percent of the money you spend on food and supplements should go for protein.

I also put a very high priority on supplementing my glutamine stores. Whenever you put physical or mental stress on your body, your muscles are robbed of the intramuscular stores of glutamine, which is essential for the proper use of protein.[2] In other words, any anxiety you feel, and even weight training itself, can keep you from building muscle as quickly and efficiently as possible when you don't have enough glutamine available.

Creatine can produce a dramatic, quality weight gain in the shortest time, probably more than any other supplement on the market. When I first started taking creatine, I gained 19 pounds in the first three weeks! Many other drug-free trainees have experienced similar results. Creatine aids in the turnover of adenosine triphosphate (ATP), which is the compound in your muscle cells that generates muscle power. Higher levels of creatine in your system help you train harder and longer. Although it has not yet been scientifically documented, experts believe that creatine also helps your muscles retain more fluids, giving you a larger, fuller appearance.

Proper timing of doses is very important to the overall effectiveness of certain supplements. There are a lot of opinions on the subject, and you'll need to monitor your progress to determine the way the timing of different supplements specifically affects you.

There are a few simple rules that apply to most of us, however. First of all, take high-quality supplements within two hours after intense workouts. That's when your body most needs the assistance. Also, it's far better to ingest supplements in smaller quantities more frequently throughout the day than less often in larger doses—just as it is with your food.

Skip La Cour.

and grow after that awesome workout is significantly more important than the workout itself.

As I walk to my car after an outstanding workout, I remind myself that the next 22 to 23 hours of my day are critical to packing on the size I'm determined to get—so critical, in fact, that I won't even start the drive home until I've taken my postworkout supplements.

I keep a large plastic container in the trunk of my car that holds glutamine, vitamins C and E, beta-carotene, and a bottle of whey protein. I take 5 grams of glutamine, 3,000 milligrams of vitamin C, 800 international units (IU) of vitamin E, and 50,000 IU of beta-carotene. The glutamine improves the nitrogen balance in my muscles, counteracts the decline of protein synthesis, and spares the free glutamine in the tissue—all of which was destroyed during my intense training session.[3,4] I also take the combination of vitamins C, E, and beta-carotene to combat the free radicals that were produced. At that point, immediately after my workout, my body is primed for protein synthesis.[5] I then drink two servings, or 48 grams, of whey protein in one quart of water.

When I get home from my workout, I immediately eat a meal that includes a good source of complex carbohydrates, such as oatmeal, Cream of Wheat, or Cream of Rice.

Tom Platz.

Try using the different supplements separately so they don't compete in your system. Recent studies have shown that glutamine and creatine actually fight each other for transportation to the muscle cells. That means you get the benefits of one *or* the other, but not both. One will be excreted from your body. That's not only inefficient but also quite costly. I always take glutamine and creatine one hour apart.

POSTWORKOUT SUPPLEMENTATION IS CRITICAL

Although training heavily and with intensity is an important step toward building muscle mass, it's only the beginning of the process. What you do to help your body rebuild itself

Tatiana Anderson.

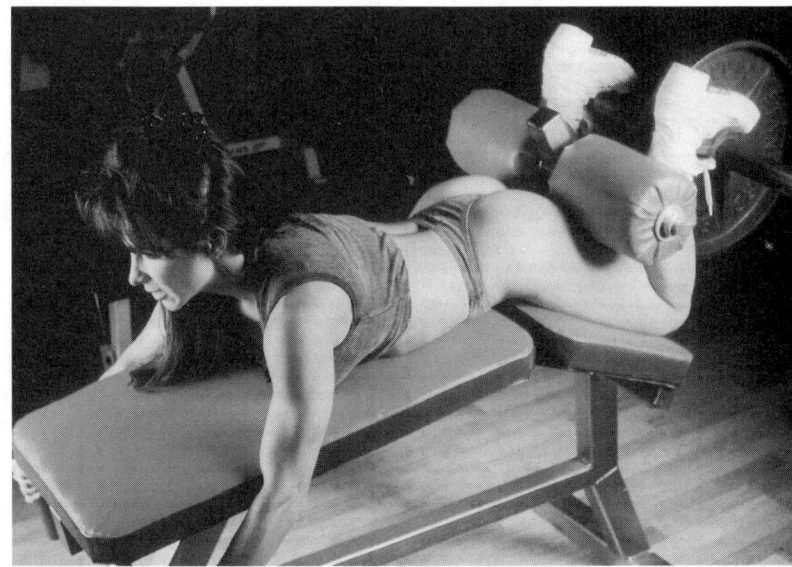

Jean-Pierre Fux.

KEEP A POSITIVE ATTITUDE

I conducted a survey at my website in which I asked a variety of questions about the value of supplements. Many of the 300 participants were very skeptical, to say the least, that supplement companies offer products that contain what's promised on the label.

Nonetheless, the average respondent reported spending $100 a month on supplements and rated them 7.6 out of 10 in terms of their effectiveness. Based on the survey results, I'd say that bodybuilders desperately want to believe that supplements will do the job for them—but they have some serious doubts. When you think about it, how can you really know for sure whether the supplement will work or that the manufacturer will deliver on its promises? You can't. It's simply a matter of trust.

One complaint I often hear from jaded bodybuilders is "Of course that magazine is going to promote that supplement line! It's their product!" Try looking at it this way. If the magazine is a high-quality publication that contains advanced scientific information—and you buy it regularly because it helps you meet your bodybuilding goals—why wouldn't the people publishing it be consistent in their ethics and produce outstanding supplements as well? Sure, they want you to buy their supplements. They're extremely proud of what they have to offer you!

Here are my suggestions for getting the most out of your supplement purchases:

- Buy supplements only from companies that you feel are well established. If the company has been around for a long time, then it must be doing something right. If you see the same ad for the same product month after month and year after year, you can be sure that the product sells very well. Supplement companies don't spend their money on advertising products that bodybuilders don't buy. That just doesn't make good business sense.

Jean-Pierre Fux.

Will Willis.

- Listen to successful bodybuilders you know and trust to hear what they have to say about a company and its products.
- Document your progress when trying new supplements.
- Stay positive and have faith in your purchases. The mind is an incredible tool. We've all heard about the placebo effect. That's what happens when patients, given an ineffective drug, believe in the drug so it works anyway. The idea has also been demonstrated in reverse. Patients were given a potent drug, but told it was only a placebo, and then the drug didn't work. Don't take the chance of letting a negative attitude make your work ineffective.

When you augment your nutritional plan with advanced, research-based supplements, you can create an ideal environment for building muscle mass and keeping your bodyfat low. If you successfully add those strategies to the motivation, training, and nutritional

Michael Francois.

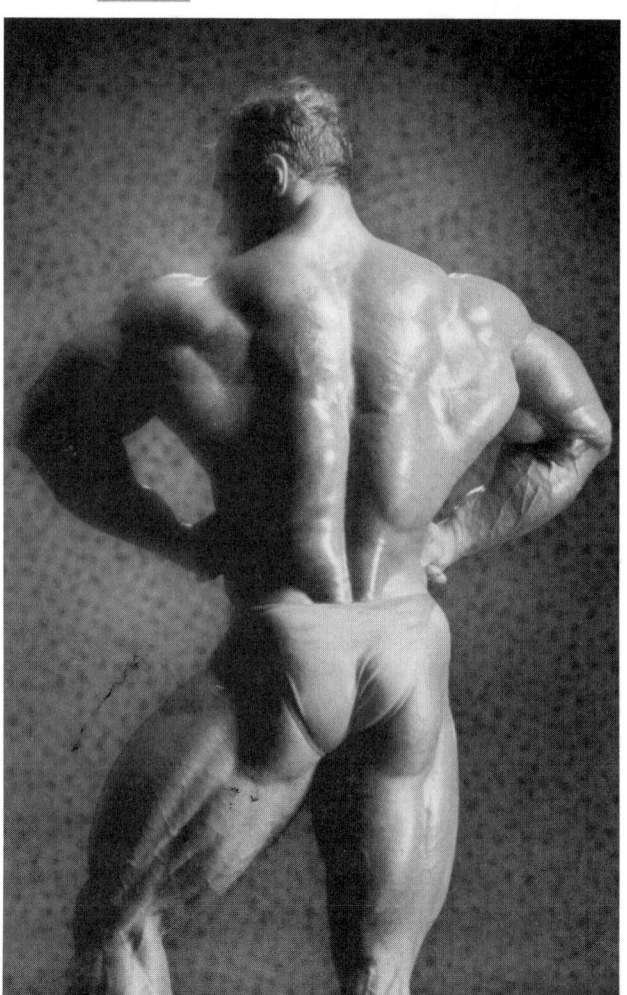

approaches that I have discussed in recent issues of *Ironman*, you'll be amazed at the quality physique you can achieve.

SKIP LA COUR'S TOP FIVE SUPPLEMENTS

In order of priority, here are my recommendations:

1. **High-quality whey protein.** I believe that whey protein is the most efficient and effective protein for building muscle. Be careful, however: you get what you pay for!

2. **Meal replacements.** For any bodybuilder who feels nutritionally challenged at times (which probably includes most of us), meal replacements have made it a whole lot easier to live the bodybuilding lifestyle. Meal replacements provide the quality protein you need to build muscle while offering moderate amounts of carbohydrates and very low amounts of fat. Now you have far fewer reasons not to eat the way you should if you expect to grow.

3. **Glutamine.** I'm giving glutamine higher priority than creatine? That's right. Like protein, glutamine is extremely effective, although the benefits are not as obvious as they are with other supplements. Glutamine is probably the most significant amino acid for bodybuilders. It has multi-faceted benefits, such as a greater-than-400-percent increase in growth-hormone release, and it's the primary component in your effort to negate the catabolic effects of training.

4. **Creatine.** It's probably the most heralded bodybuilding supplement in recent times. I imagine that's because creatine brings most of us size and strength almost immediately after we start using it—making it an instant winner in a society that craves instant gratification. A constituent of skeletal

muscle tissue, creatine is phosphory-lated to store energy used for muscular contraction.

5. **Multivitamin.** This pill is a not-so-glamorous but essential supplement that provides assurance that you're getting all the nutrients you need every day. In order for your body to perform at peak levels, you must consume a wide array of important nutrients.

WHEN TO TAKE YOUR SUPPLEMENTS

High-quality protein supplement. Take it after every meal of regular food.

Meal replacement. Take one as a meal two to three hours after each regular meal of food.

Glutamine. Take it immediately after your workout.

Multivitamin. Take it after breakfast and also in the evening.

Creatine. Take it one hour after your workout and at noon.

Antioxidants. Take vitamin C (3,000 milligrams), beta-carotene (50,000 IU), and vitamin E (800 IU) immediately after your workout.

Vanadyl sulfate. Take it three times a day. Vanadyl sulfate uses key nutrients that medical studies have shown increase whole-body glucose disposal.

Pro-hormones. Take them twice a day. Pro-hormones are supplements designed to boost your testosterone levels. The more circulating testosterone you have in your system, the more lean muscle mass you're going to build. Check with your competitive bodybuilding organization, however, as these supplements may soon be banned—not because they're harmful or violate any state and federal laws but because they can appear in a urine test as illegal

Mike Ashley.

drugs. Pro-hormones are banned by the International Olympic Committee.

References

1. Colgan, M. 1993. *Optimum Sports Nutrition.* New York: Advanced Research Press.
2. Chesley et al. 1992. Changes in human muscle protein synthesis after resistance training. *Journal of Applied Physiology.* 1383–1388.
3. Matthews, D. E., and A. Battezzati. 1993. *Current opinion.* General Surgeon. 72–77.
4. Falduto, M. T., A. P. Young, and R. C. Hickson. 1992. *American Journal of Physiology.* December: E1157–E1163.
5. Hickson, R. C., S. M. Czerwinski, and L. E. Wegrzyn. 1995. *American Journal of Physiology.* April: E730–E734.

Lee Priest.

Chapter 2

THE INSULIN/MUSCLE-MASS CONNECTION

BY ELIOT JORDAN

Some people refer to insulin as the most anabolic hormone of them all, including testosterone, growth hormone, and insulin-like growth factor (IGF-1). To many people, however, insulin is primarily associated with two types of diabetes. Type 1, also called insulin-dependent diabetes mellitus, is characterized by a failure to secrete insulin in response to insulin-provoking nutrients, such as carbohydrates. Type 2, or noninsulin-dependent diabetes, is associated with either a failure to secrete enough insulin or a decrease of insulin cell receptors.

Since the symptoms for both types of diabetes include elevated blood glucose levels, or hyperglycemia, insulin is most associated with carbohydrate metabolism. Insulin, however, is an all-purpose storage hormone that not only promotes storage of carbohydrates as glycogen but also plays an integral role in bodyfat accretion and muscle protein synthesis.

The latter effect is the subject of debate in scientific circles. Some researchers say that insulin exerts merely a permissive effect on muscle-cell protein synthesis, while others believe it's anticatabolic in that it appears to prevent excessive breakdown of muscle protein. Still another popular hypothesis is that insulin directly stimulates muscle protein synthesis, an anabolic action.

Much of the confusion on the issue of how insulin affects muscle is based on variously designed studies. Just as anabolic steroids work better if supplied with an anabolic stimulus in the form of exercise, the same appears to be the case with insulin. In other words, taking insulin will not promote muscular growth unless accompanied by a certain type of exercise. The type of exercise required is weight training.

A study published in a 1996 issue of the *American Journal of Physiology* underscores this notion. The study involved rats placed on a weight-training protocol, as compared with sedentary rats. The purpose of the study was to find out how insulin affected muscle protein synthesis and to clear up some of the confusion regarding the hormone's role as either a protein-synthesis promoter or an anticatabolic substance.

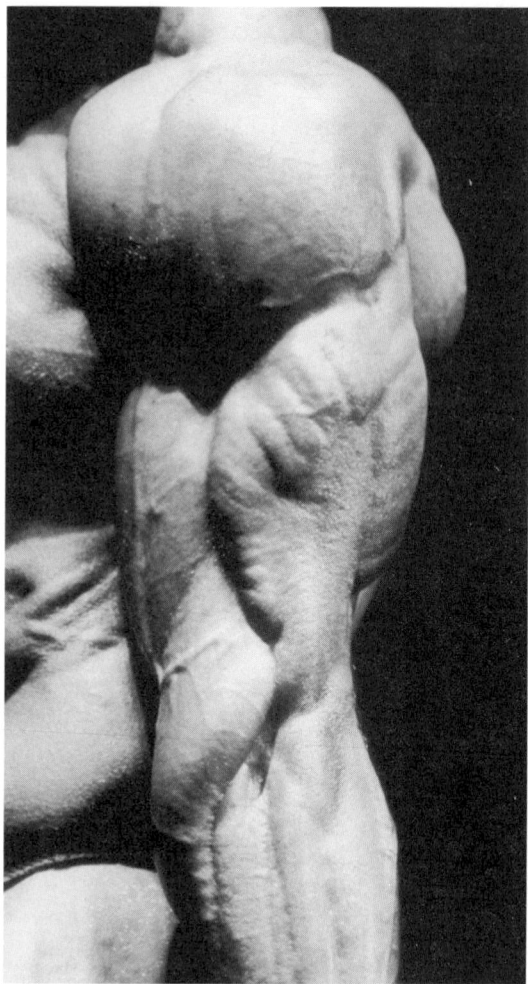

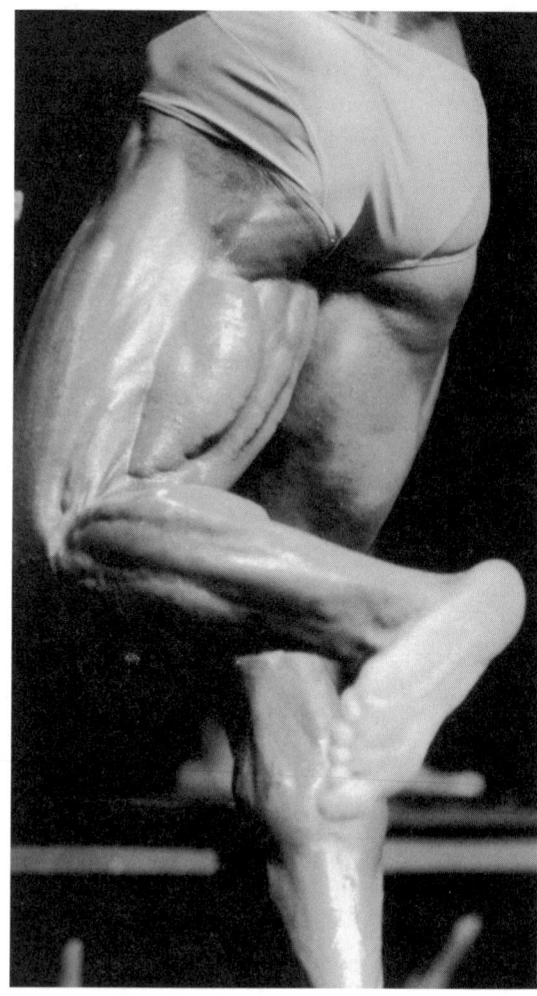

As expected, giving insulin to nonexercising rats didn't affect muscle protein synthesis in any way. Nor did giving it to aerobic-exercising rats provide any anabolic stimulus. Providing insulin to weight-training rats, however, did promote increased muscle protein synthesis—but only in the exercised muscles.

The researchers point out that past studies showing only an anticatabolic effect of insulin on muscle were incomplete because they involved either sedentary or aerobic-exercising rats. Apparently, there has to be a minimum level of muscle contractile activity that can be produced only by resistance exercise, such as weight training, for insulin to promote muscle protein synthesis.

The study also examined the effects of insulin on both fast-twitch and slow-twitch muscle fibers. Slow-twitch fibers are most associated with endurance exercise, while fast-twitch fibers are involved in anaerobic exercise, such as bodybuilding. Fast-twitch fibers are far more prone to muscular growth than are slow-twitch ones.

The study showed that insulin is absolutely required for muscle protein synthesis in

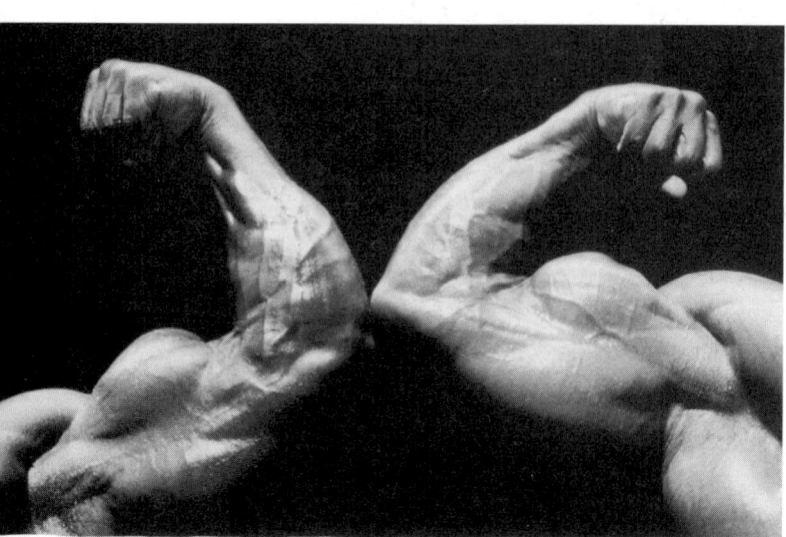

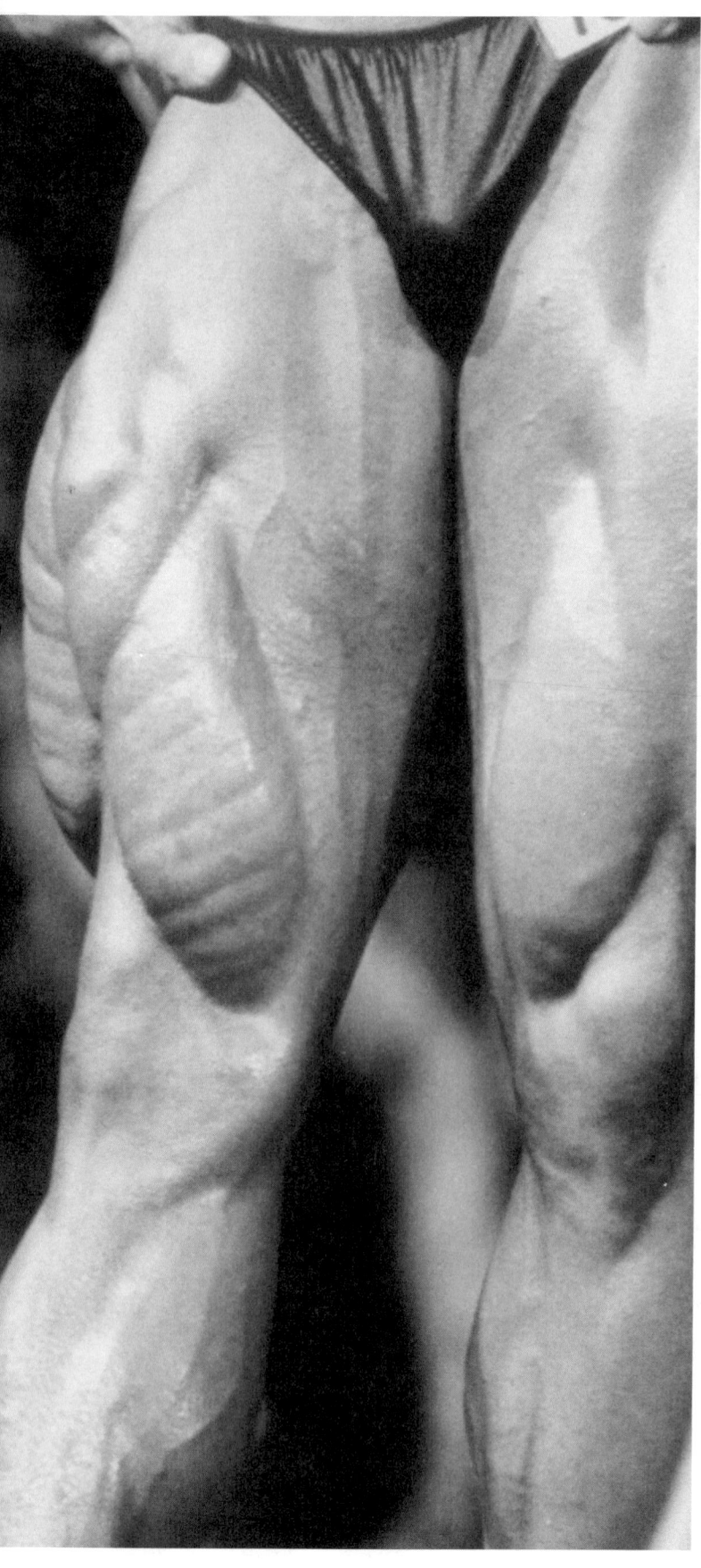

fast-twitch fibers but isn't a necessity for slow-twitch fibers. This result most likely relates to the greater protein synthesis occurring in the fast-twitch fibers. Thus, insulin works hand in hand with resistance exercise to promote increased muscular growth.

I recall talking with Tim Belknap, the 1981 Mr. America, who has had type 1 diabetes since he was 13. He told me that shortly after he began taking insulin to control his diabetes, he started bodybuilding and quickly gained 30 pounds of pure muscle. He attributes his rapid initial muscle gains to the insulin but is quick to advise nondiabetic bodybuilders *against* using insulin for muscle-building purposes because of the hormone's likely side effects.

Belknap is referring to the possible side effects of indiscriminate insulin use. Since insulin rapidly decreases levels of blood glucose, it can produce a state of hypoglycemia potent enough to put you in a coma. That's especially true if you're also on a carbohydrate-restricted diet.

On the other hand, the anabolic trio of insulin, growth hormone, and anabolic steroids is considered by some to be the reason for the current 250-plus-pound behemoths you see competing in professional bodybuilding. Having conferred with many of these competitors, however, I can tell you that there's no standard insulin regimen; the doses and even the type of insulin are determined by either guesswork or trial-and-error experimentation.

Several bodybuilders have nearly become comatose because of insulin use. In most cases this occurred just before a contest, when the insulin was injected as a means of increasing muscle glycogen storage. The supposed purpose of this technique is a kind of high-tech carbohydrate loading that makes the muscle appear fuller at the contest. Insulin helps with this because it turns on the rate-limiting enzyme for muscle glycogen synthesis, glycogen synthetase. Unfortunately, several of insulin's physiological properties make this technique very tricky.

You must know precisely how to balance insulin use with carbohydrate intake. As noted earlier, taking large amounts of insulin without concurrently taking in carbohydrates is a ticket to Comaville. Another problem is that insulin stimulates water and sodium retention, which is exactly what a bodybuilder seeking that ripped appearance doesn't want. There's also insulin's effect in promoting bodyfat accretion—a look that's definitely *out* in bodybuilding contests.

Perhaps the most prudent way to deal with insulin is through natural means. You can potentiate insulin's effects without fear of side effects by increasing your intake of the trace mineral chromium. Since the body absorbs only about 5 to 10 percent of oral chromium, you can take 200 to 600 micrograms a day in divided doses without fear of detrimental effects. Vanadyl sulfate exerts an independent insulin-like action, particularly in regard to muscle glycogen storage; however, its effects on protein synthesis are still subject to debate.

Taking a combination protein-and-carbohydrate drink right after training boosts insulin output 37 percent higher than consuming carbohydrates alone. While some advise actually drinking this combo during a workout, the advantages are few—and the possible side effects, such as bloating, are more likely. A postworkout drink containing about 50 grams of protein and 50 to 100 grams of carbohydrate should do the trick in providing the needed insulin anabolic effect after a workout.

Jean-Pierre Fux.

Kevin Hall.

Chapter 3

CALCIUM— THE MISSING MINERAL

BY DANIEL CURTIS

Bodybuilders eat well. In fact, they eat very well. A study published in the *Journal of Sports Medicine and Physical Fitness* (29:63–70, 1989) reported that "all of the bodybuilders' vitamin/mineral intakes exceeded the RDAS with the exception of one nutrient." If you guessed that nutrient was calcium, you're right. The men met only 54 percent of the U.S. recommended daily allowance (RDA) for calcium, and the women met only 60 percent. Another study, this one published in the *Journal of the American Dietetic Association* (90:962–967, 1990), reported that women "had remarkably deficient calcium intake, despite an adequate energy intake."

Why do bodybuilders come up short on calcium? Primarily because they associate dairy products with fat. Since fat equals a smooth physique, they avoid dairy products— and the result is a dietary deficiency of calcium.

Should you be concerned about that deficiency? Probably. Among calcium's many functions—which include building and main-taining bones and teeth, promoting the transmission of nerve impulses, helping blood clot when necessary, and regulating blood pressure—is its ability to aid in muscle contraction.

According to the textbook *Nutrition in Health and Disease,* "Calcium has a vital role in the contraction and relaxation of muscle. Its entrance into the muscle cell as a result of nerve stimulation sets in motion the biochemical processes which cause the proteins myosin and actin to be drawn together, thus contracting the muscle cells by making them shorter and thicker." Such a contribution makes this nutrient more than just a little important to the bodybuilder.

The RDA for calcium is 800 milligrams for men and women, although recently, some experts have begun advising 1,200 to 1,500 milligrams for women in an effort to prevent osteoporosis.

The easiest way to meet calcium needs is to include dairy products in the diet. All dairy products now come in fat-free form. Most

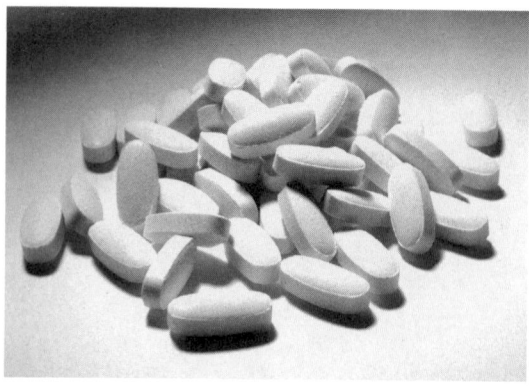

people are familiar with nonfat milk, but yogurt, cottage cheese, sliced cheeses, cream cheese, and sour cream are all available in fat-free versions as well. While such fat-free products have a lot fewer calories, the calcium content stays the same. Eight ounces of nonfat milk supply 300 milligrams of calcium, the same as eight ounces of regular, whole milk. Eight ounces of nonfat yogurt and one ounce

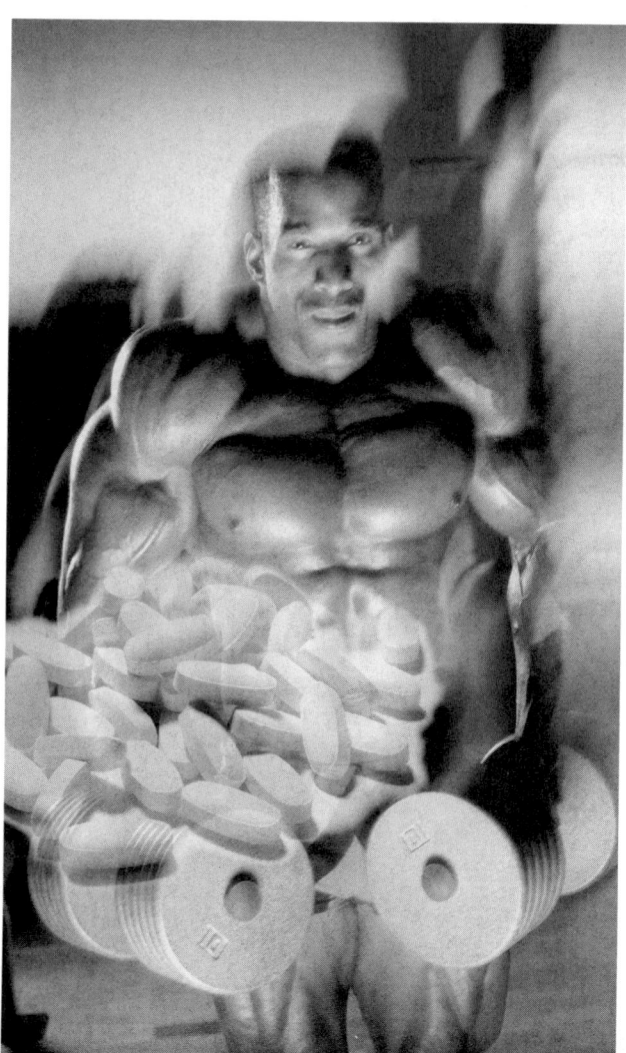

of nonfat cheese also supply 300 milligrams of calcium each. That's close to half your daily requirement. A half cup of nonfat sour cream supplies 120 milligrams of calcium and minimal calories, and two tablespoons of nonfat cream cheese supply 25 milligrams. Of course, other milk-based foods, such as cream soups, custards, ice cream, whipped cream, and half-and-half, contain considerable amounts of calcium as well, but they also have considerable amounts of fat and calories, which would be detrimental to a muscle builder's goals.

As easy as it is to reach the requirement for calcium by eating dairy products, some people won't use them at all, nonfat or not. They believe that pasteurization destroys all the nutrients or that antibiotics and chemicals are passed from the animal to the milk. Regardless of these concerns and whether they're justified, the body needs calcium.

Some people simply cannot tolerate dairy products. They suffer from lactose intolerance, which means their bodies cannot break down the milk sugar, or lactose, because they have inadequate levels of the enzyme lactase. If lactose isn't broken down by lactase in the small intestine, it travels farther down the intestine, where it doesn't belong. There it reacts with the bacteria and causes gas, cramping, and diarrhea. If you suffer from lactose intolerance, there's probably a simple solution. You can take lactase tablets before eating dairy products. Another helpful method is to add lactase drops to liquid milk, mix well, and let it react overnight; it will break down the lactose for you so your body can handle it.

If you can't or won't use dairy products but wish to meet your daily calcium needs, there are nondairy sources of calcium, including broccoli (90 milligrams per half cup), spinach (120 milligrams per half cup), kale (50 milligrams per half cup), turnip greens (100 milligrams per half cup), and tofu (130 milligrams per half cup, raw). These vegetables not only provide calcium, but they're rich in other nutrients, too, and have few calories. Salmon and sardines supply calcium if you eat the bones.

Dave Liberman.

Supplementation is another option. Unfortunately, you won't find much calcium in a multiple vitamin. For instance, Centrum, which is a good, complete multivitamin and mineral supplement, contains only 162 milligrams of calcium per tablet, which is not even 20 percent of the RDA. Finding a multivitamin that has more calcium crammed into it means you're going to be looking at a tablet that even a python would have a hard time swallowing. Your best bet is to use an additional calcium supplement.

How do you select a good one? Calcium needs vitamin D to help the body absorb it. If you're taking a daily multivitamin, you're already getting all the vitamin D you need—most such pills contain 100 percent of the RDA—and can select a supplement that is straight calcium. If you aren't taking a multivitamin, you need a supplement that contains calcium plus vitamin D.

As to the best type of calcium, calcium carbonate is the form of choice. It contains 40 percent calcium by weight, which is more than other forms such as calcium lactate or calcium gluconate, and it is the least expensive. Take the tablet on an empty stomach with eight ounces of liquid for best absorption. If it upsets your stomach, take it with a meal and you should be able to tolerate it. Read the label for the amount of calcium per tablet and set your dose according to the amount you're already getting from your diet.

Turn your eating habits from great to even greater by getting more of the one nutrient that bodybuilders don't get enough of—calcium.

Shawn Ray.

Chapter 4

STAY HUNGRY: WHEN TO EAT—AND NOT TO EAT—FOR BEST MUSCLE-BUILDING RESULTS

BY RON J. CLARK

Have you ever heard the phrase "Stay hungry"? If you're a longtime bodybuilding fan, chances are you have. The Austrian oak himself, Arnold Schwarzenegger, made this phrase popular—so popular, in fact, that one of the first films he ever appeared in was called *Stay Hungry*. Once again, it seems, the bodybuilding community was a step ahead of the scientists! It turns out that hunger pangs can generally be relieved by a bout of moderate-to-intense resistance exercise and that training performance is enhanced when you train on an empty stomach.

Consider the practice of training hungry a vital tool in all resistance-exercise programs. In the simplest of terms, resistance exercise and eating don't mix. Moreover, hunger pangs alone shouldn't dictate when you eat. In fact, the sensation of hunger has absolutely nothing to do with intelligently timed eating.

For example, many experts consider the postexercise meal to be the most important meal of the day, as it's essential that trainees get recovery energy as soon as possible following a workout. The replacement of expended energy and the maintenance of a positive nitrogen balance are critical. Ideally, you should eat that meal within a very short period after your workout. There's another reason to eat after you train: exercise soothes hunger pangs. In other words, you're not hungry, which makes it an excellent time to eat.

You should consider hunger pains to be a preliminary starvation warning—and something you want to avoid. The faster the metabolism, the more often the warning. In general, when you stick with an optimal nutrition program, you shouldn't feel hunger pangs—except just prior to the workout—as you should be eating frequently enough to avoid them.

Training hungry also has biological value. When you eat, the food travels to the small intestine, where almost all digestion occurs. The conversion and use of broken-down nutrients becomes a priority to the body. In order to transport these newly absorbed nutrients to various organs and tissues, the blood

Rich Piana.

vessels in and around muscle tissues *constrict*, while the vessels in and around the digestive organs *dilate*. This forces blood *away from* muscles and toward the digestive system, minimizing oxygen and nutrients going to the muscles. Imagine what happens when you eat just before you train. Digestion occurs at the same time you perform the activity. This results in a tug-of-war between your muscles and digestive system, both desperately in need of increased blood flow.

What happens as a result? Exercise is more taxing and digestion is compromised. Neither activity receives adequate oxygen and nutrients. What are typical signs of this tug-of-war? Excessive rapid breathing, abnormally high exercise heart rate, nausea, and dizziness. The degree of discomfort and severity of the symptoms vary according to your intensity. When you experience any of them, you should stop training.

Kevin Hall.

Henrik Thamasian.

Barry Kabov and Frankie Lee Wright.

GUIDELINES TO PLAN YOUR TRAINING MEAL

Obviously, you have to eat. Here are some considerations for planning the last meal you eat before you train:

1. Eat the right types of food. Proteins and lots of light-carb foods, like fruit, are appropriate. Generally speaking, select complex carbs that are easily digested to ensure there's minimal digestion going on when you start working out.
2. Make your preworkout meal small. There's no reason to ingest more than 500 calories before a resistance-training workout, since the majority of energy you use will come from your muscle tissues. This low number of calories should minimize digestion when you're working out, thus freeing more blood for the purpose of transporting nutrients and oxygen to working muscles.

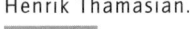

Henrik Thamasian.

3. Since it's important to include protein in every meal, and since protein takes somewhat longer to assimilate, timing when you eat is also among the most important considerations in planning a preworkout meal. Eat the preworkout meal about two to three hours before your scheduled workout. In most cases, this interval should provide plenty of time for the absorption of the small amount of food.

In summary, hunger should never dictate meal planning. You will greatly improve your workout performance when you train hungry. By eating frequently—and intelligently—you eliminate hunger during the day, except possibly just before you train.

Flex Wheeler.

Bruce Patterson.

Chapter 5

BREAKFAST OF SMART CHAMPIONS

BY ELLINGTON DARDEN, PH.D.

There's a line in a Kurt Vonnegut book that always struck me as being right on the money. It said (in paraphrase) that everything we say, do, or think is a by-product of what we ate for breakfast this morning. Vonnegut, although probably not a student of neuroendocrinology, seems to have understood that our brains function through a bunch of chemical interactions.

Teach members of a species of flatworm called *planaria* to respond to a stimulus of light, grind them up, and feed them to ignorant planarians, and the ignorant eaters will respond to the stimulus in the same way. Why? Chemicals—the chemicals involved in learning.

Although I'm not proposing you put Dorian Yates in a log shredder and eat him with ketchup to assimilate his bodybuilding knowledge, the point stands. Everything is controlled by the brain, and I'm not talking just about memory, feelings of well-being, or energy. I'm also talking about motor-unit recruitment. A brain that produces optimum amounts of the chemicals called neurotransmitters in all probability recruits lots of muscle fibers, and that ultimately leads to greater strength and more productive workouts.

European bodybuilders and strength athletes have been manipulating these naturally occurring chemicals for a long time. They have known that certain pharmaceuticals effectively increase levels of stimulatory neurotransmitters, but they used them haphazardly, taking whatever was available. If used correctly, however, the nutrients energize their users, pushing them to unparalleled strength and muscle gains without any of the negative side effects of illegal amphetamines or other uppers.

Information of the Europeans' intriguing practice only recently reached the United States. Unfortunately, a few U.S. supplement companies seized the idea and ran with it, throwing together a hodgepodge of potentially stimulatory nutrients with little or no regard for how the chemicals act together. Those everything-but-the-kitchen-sink concoctions have made some bodybuilders sleepy, grumpy, and maybe even a little dopey—hardly the feelings you want as you step under the squat rack.

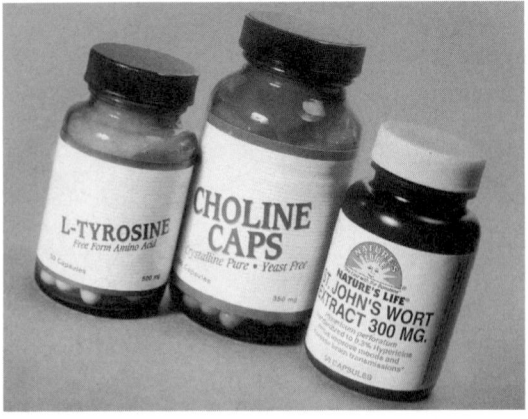

A LITTLE SCIENCE

The nervous and endocrine systems are closely linked. Glands throughout your body release hormones, but most of the glands are activated by nerves. Conversely, the endocrine glands control some of the functions of the nervous system. The endocrine system uses hormones to send messages, whereas the neurocrine system uses neurotransmitters. Although there are some 50 neurotransmitters, only about 10 are involved in most brain-cell communication. You might be familiar with adrenaline, noradrenaline, acetylcholine, serotonin, and dopamine. The first two, now known as epinephrine and norepinephrine, elevate mood, alertness, and even assertiveness. Acetylcholine seems to facilitate memory and help control movement, while serotonin causes drowsiness and relaxation. Dopamine is essential for both sexual arousal and coordination.[2,3] All of the neurotransmitters, with the exception of acetylcholine, are made from amino acids supplied by dietary protein.

The cellular units that use these chemicals are called neurons, and there are probably more than a billion of them in the brain alone. Each of those neurons is, in effect, an electrical conduit that receives or transmits signals that cross a space called a *synapse*. The actual transmission is mediated by the neurotransmitter chemicals.

An average neuron has several thousand synaptic junctions. Theoretically, if you have optimal levels of neurotransmitters, you're more energetic or dynamic. If you have subpar levels, you could suffer from depression, a lack of energy, or even diminished muscle motor-unit recruitment. Whether you're lifting a weight, taking a step, or moving your eyes across this page, the muscle actions are controlled largely by neurotransmitters.

If, for instance, you're trying to curl a 40-pound dumbbell, you need a certain number of muscle cells, or motor units, to do it. Let's say your supply of neurotransmitters is as low as that of a three-toed sloth, either as a natural side effect of aging or from the lack of a

Arne List.

Johnny Stewart.

proper diet. You might not be able to activate enough muscle cells to accomplish the lift. If you could somehow increase the number of neurotransmitters, you might be able to recruit enough fibers to lift the weight.

The effects of caffeine, amphetamines, and other central nervous system stimulants have long been known. They include improved focus,[6] greater alertness, and even a decreased sensitivity to pain.[8] Several studies have shown that subjects had substantial increases in strength after taking such stimulants.[4,5] The chemicals, however, have obvious problems. Amphetamines are addictive, not to mention illegal, and have far-reaching effects on behavior. Caffeine is also addictive but doesn't have the negative effects of amphetamines. It can cause feelings of jitteriness when used to excess, though. None of the stimulants work by increasing the brain's neurotransmitters naturally.

Mike Ashley.

Mike Ashley.

counteracts the stimulatory effects of the amino acid tyrosine, which in large amounts causes the brain to produce norepinephrine.

People with chronically low levels of serotonin are often clinically depressed. Certain antidepressants, such as Prozac or Zoloft, work by elevating natural levels of serotonin. That's also how the herb Saint-John's-wort works. Such compounds are called monoamine oxidase inhibitors, which means that they keep the brain from breaking down serotonin, so the levels stay high—and so do you. The trouble is that none of them addresses the root of the problem: none increases production of neurotransmitters. They just cause a temporary increase in already existing supplies of the chemicals. Furthermore, they gradually become ineffective with repeated use.

Wurtman's later experiments showed that dietary choline could actually increase levels of the neurotransmitter acetylcholine, which improved the test scores of student volunteers on memory tests, and subsequent studies have supported those results.[7] It seems fairly conclusive that diet actually influences brain levels of neurotransmitters. It seems reasonable to assume that certain chemicals, taken as supplements, could improve brain function and athletic performance, including strength.

A LITTLE HISTORY

Until the 1970s most scientists believed that the brain controlled the levels of neurotransmitters, regardless of diet. Then Massachusetts Institute of Technology Professor Richard Wurtman, along with some colleagues, showed that even a single meal can influence the levels of those chemicals. A meal rich in protein can encourage high epinephrine and norepinephrine levels, which would result in increased alertness and more energy.

Wurtman's early experiments involved tryptophan. They showed that when large amounts of that amino acid cross the blood-brain barrier, the brain produces more serotonin, which has a calming effect. That

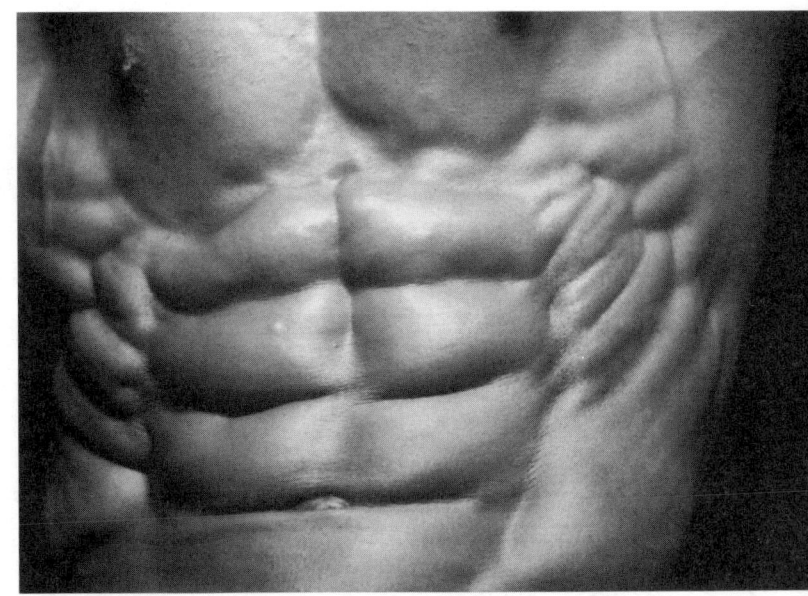

Ahmo Hight.

Roger Applewhite.

WHAT MAKES A GOOD NEUROTRANSMITTER SUPPLEMENT?

An ideal supplement would contain a hefty amount of the amino acid tyrosine. This compound converts to dopamine, norepinephrine, and epinephrine, substances known collectively as catecholamines. It's estimated that about 90 percent of the brain's catecholamines are synthesized directly from natural tyrosine. Some researchers have treated certain forms of depression with tyrosine. There's some clinical evidence and a lot of anecdotal evidence that taking 2 to 3 grams of tyrosine before a workout, on an empty stomach, can enhance alert-

ness and performance in the gym, even increasing strength dramatically.

A tyrosine-related rise in dopamine levels might also be beneficial in that, as dopamine levels drop as a result of aging, levels of prolactin go up. Increases in the hormone prolactin are accompanied by decreases in testosterone levels.

An effective supplementation product would also increase levels of acetylcholine, which improves memory and, apparently, the mind-muscle connection. About 1 gram of a supplement known as phosphatidylcholine would lead to increased levels of acetylcholine.[1] Some people take it as a brain-enhancing drug, and the effects have reportedly lasted up

James Demelo.

to 30 days in some cases, which would support the idea that it increases neurotransmitter sites. There are other ingredients that would enhance a supplement's effectiveness. Serine is an amino acid that's known to play a role in regulating brain glucose metabolism, in addition to increasing neurotransmitter receptor sites. It's also thought to enhance the enzymes involved in neurotransmitter release. Obviously, using the three compounds together should be quite useful.

Other possibly effective, legal, and apparently safe ingredients might be the well-known herb ginkgo biloba and a brain nutrient known as DMAE. The latter is thought to also increase acetylcholine levels, while the former is said to increase blood flow to the brain.

Currently, the only company that's close to developing such a well-thought-out product is Biotest Laboratories. The preliminary results look exciting, and company CEO Tim Patterson is optimistic. "In the past," he says, "most research involving tyrosine and other neurotransmitter products has centered largely on behavior modification. The results were sometimes inconclusive because the effect of a given nutrient on a neuron often depends on the neuron's firing rate. This means that maybe only people with a dopamine-depleting condition—like Parkinson's disease—would respond to tyrosine or other brain-stimulatory supplements.

"There is, however, one area that previous researchers haven't really considered—vigorous exercise. Vigorous exercise like strength training probably also increases the firing rate of neurons. Therefore supplemental tyrosine should increase strength, performance, and muscle size, as a result of enhanced motor-unit recruitment."

Obviously, the entire research area of neurotransmitters is both complicated and exciting. If we can really improve our performance in the gym (or boardroom, schoolroom, or bedroom, for that matter), then Biotest's research may put a whole new face on bodybuilding.

Paul DeMayo.

Flex Wheeler.

References

1. Crook, T., et al. 1992. Effects of phosphatidylserine in Alzheimer's disease. *Psychopharmacol Bull.* 28:61–66.

2. Dean, W., et al. 1993. *Smart Drugs II, the Next Generation.* Petaluma, CA: Smart Publications.

3. Dean, W., and J. Morgenthaler. 1990. *Smart Drugs and Nutrients.* Petaluma, CA: Smart Publications.

4. Hurst, P. M., et al. 1968. The effects of D-amphetamine and chlordiazepoxide upon strength and estimated strength. *Ergonomics.* 11:47–52.

5. Jackman, M., et al. 1996. Metabolic, catecholamine, and endurance responses to caffeine during intense exercise. *Journal of Applied Physiology.* 81:1658–1663.

6. Klinkhammer, P., et al. 1990. Effect of phosphatidylserine on cerebral glucose metabolism in Alzheimer's disease. *Dementia.* 1:197–201.

7. Lino, A., et al. 1992. Psycho-functional changes in attention and learning under the action of L-acetylcarnitine in 17 young subjects: A pilot study of its use in mental deterioration. *Clin. Ter.* (Italy). 140:569–573.

8. Percy, E. C. 1978. Ergogenic aids in athletics, medicine, and science. *Sports and Exercise.* 10:298–303.

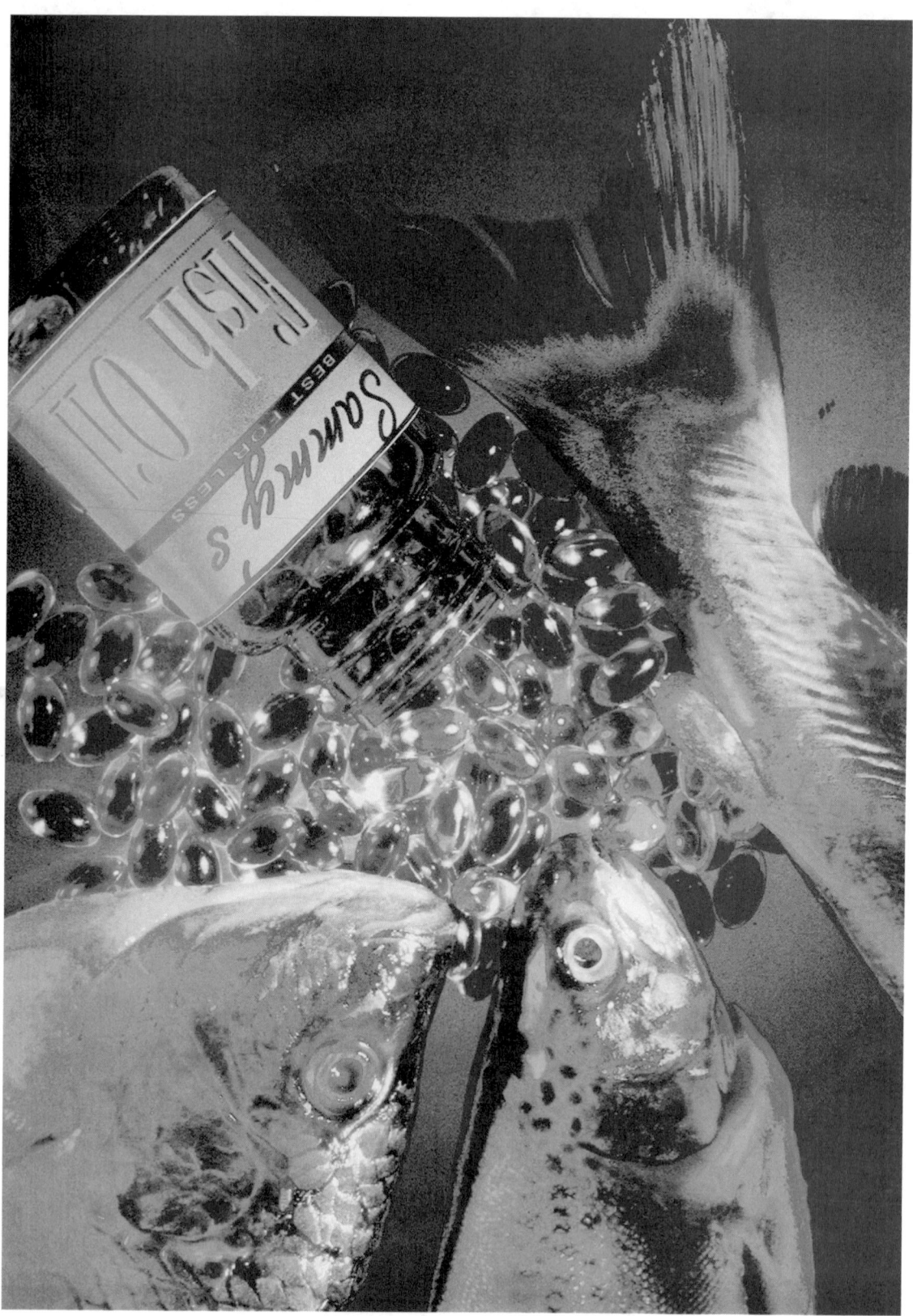

Chapter 6

THE REAL SCOOP ON PROTEIN

BY GEORGE L. REDMIN, PH.D.

According to Francis Nettl, M.D., former director of exercise and rehabilitative medicine for the U.S. Navy, "A high biologically active protein source is considerably more apt to prevent catabolic conditions because of its superior absorption and retention ability."[1] If you're a professional bodybuilder, a pro bodybuilding wannabe, or just an average Joe or Jane who's poring over loads of information trying to determine if you need to add protein to enhance your workout regimen, Dr. Nettl has expressed the issue for you in a nutshell.

The question of whether large quantities of dietary protein are necessary to optimize protein synthesis and enhance muscular hypertrophy and strength has been debated for more than one hundred years, a debate that's been fueled by extravagant claims and the many different proprietary brands of protein products available. Even now, when you hit the local gym, health club, or health-food store, you can't get any straight answers. If you look beyond the hype—and in some cases the scientific jargon—the mystery surrounding protein supplementation and how to choose the most effective products may be easier to solve. You just need a little more information.

PROTEIN 101

Proteins are the basic building blocks of life, the body's main structural components. The proteins in food are too large to be absorbed through your intestines, so they're broken down during digestion into smaller components called *amino acids*. The smaller agents are then able to penetrate the intestinal wall and are absorbed into the bloodstream after they're reassembled and used to build and maintain the body's structure. Those amino acids not used for that purpose are instead used for energy. We know of twenty-two amino acids. Eight of them are considered *essential*, meaning that the body can't make them and so they must be supplied through the diet. The other fourteen, known as *nonessential amino acids*, are made in your body. The chart on page 41 lists all the amino acids.

Sonny Schmidt.

When you look into the mirror, you're viewing protein in action. Your hair, eyes, skin, bones, heart, veins, and muscles, as well as the genes that carry your individual blueprint, are made of protein. While other food factors are important, it's protein that actually builds your muscles. Only protein gives your muscles the nitrogen necessary for growth, recovery, and repair. Nothing gives you more nitrogen than protein—not carbs, anticatabolic substances (things that slow muscle protein breakdown), fats, or even creatine and HMB.[2]

Amino Acids
Essential
Isoleucine
Leucine
Lysine
Methionine
Theronine
Tryptophan
Valine
Phenylalanine
Nonessential
Alanine
Asparagine
Arginine
Cysteine
Glutamic acid
Glycine
Histidine
Aspartic acid
Beta-hydroxy glutamic acid
Hydroxyproline
Norleucine
Proline
Serine
Tyrosine

Although there's a clear distinction between essential and nonessential amino acids, the term *nonessential* is something of a misnomer because you need all of the amino acids for superior growth. In fact, when any proteins are constructed, all of the necessary amino acids must be present at the same time.[3]

THE AMINO ACID POOL

Recent studies suggest that proper meal planning is important and that by consuming frequent meals—at least six per day—athletes can limit muscle-protein breakdown. Studying nitrogen retention and amino acid absorption into the bloodstream, scientists have found that your body lives and breathes to maintain what's called a free amino acid pool, which can be described as a small tank of amino acids that help repair and rebuild muscle tissue. When you don't take in adequate amounts of protein, however, the amino acids in the tank begin to be used up. The body starts looking for some way to refill the tank, and it breaks down existing muscle tissue to sustain the right ratios among the amino acids.

The real problem is that the free amino acid pool must be totally replaced about six times a day.[1] In fact, about 75 percent of the amino acids in the normal human adult are metabolized for the purpose of creating tissue proteins, enzymes, and protein hormones. The new proteins are needed because of the constant destruction of body proteins. Most of the amino acids that aren't used to create proteins are converted to nonprotein essential nitrogenous tissue constituents. In fact, protein itself is composed of 15 percent nitrogen. Your body constantly gives off nitrogen through waste, as well as through the hair, skin, and nails. Without ample supplies and retention of the element, you're at risk for nitrogen deficiency.[4]

Ursela Sarcev.

Porter Cottrell.

Protein Principle 1   Since protein provides the nitrogen to ensure growth, it's imperative that you maintain adequate supplies throughout the day.

PROTEIN ARITHMETIC

Given the importance of getting enough protein, the burning question for the past hundred years has been, How much is enough? The current recommendation is 0.8 gram of protein daily per kilogram of bodyweight.[5] For example, a 130-pound woman would need 47 grams of protein. To arrive at that amount, you convert the pounds into kilograms by using a conversion factor of 2.2. Here's an example:

130 pounds ÷ 2.2 = 59 kilograms
59 × 0.8 gram = 47 grams

Many researchers contend that these requirements, based on normal growth and repair, are insufficient for bodybuilding purposes. In recent years research has confirmed

that people who perform heavy resistance training require more protein than the recommendation of 0.8 gram per kilometer to maintain nitrogen balance and stimulate muscle development. Current data suggest that 1.7 to 1.8 grams of protein per kilogram of bodyweight is a more realistic figure, as illustrated in the following example. Here are figures for a 220-pound man who engages in strength and resistance training and eats six meals per day. Plug in your own weight to determine your daily intake range.

> **Step 1. Change pounds to kilograms:**
> 220 pounds ÷ 2.2 = 100 kilograms
>
> **Step 2. Multiply the weight in kilograms by 1.7 and 1.8:**
> 100 × 1.7 = 170 grams of protein per day
> 100 × 1.8 = 180 grams of protein per day
>
> **Step 3. Calculate how much protein to consume throughout the day, in this case over six meals:**
> 170 ÷ 6 = 28.3 grams of protein per meal

A word of caution

There are conflicting reports that protein intake at these higher levels poses some risks. Health officials contend that excessive amounts of proteins or amino acids unaccom-

Jean-Pierre Fux.

Jim Quinn.

Gregory Reid.

YOU ARE WHAT YOU DIGEST

According to Dr. Barry Sears, author of *Enter the Zone*, if you don't have the essential amino acids constantly entering your body, the rate of new protein formation slows down.[7] He also states that the amount of amino acids that actually enter the bloodstream is primarily determined by the digestibility of the protein source. That's due to the fact that if digestive enzymes are unable to go to the protein, the undigested portions will pass through your system without being absorbed and used by the body. What's more, with the natural daily fluctuations of amino acid levels in your bloodstream, the content of your meals can have a major impact on how well those powerful substances get to target sites, namely muscle cells.[8]

Protein Principle 2 There's mounting evidence confirming the need to include some carbohydrates at postworkout feedings to help accelerate the rate at which amino acids are shuttled into the muscle cell.[9] Current data

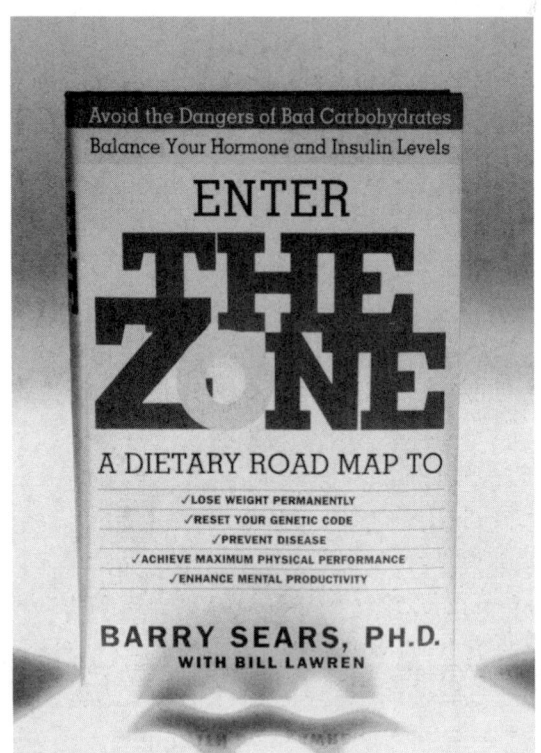

panied by proper electrolyte balance, meaning dissolved minerals in the bloodstream, saturate the body with harmful waste products, a situation caused by the incomplete conversion of protein to amino acids. As a result, the body creates uric acid, a poisonous by-product, instead of new tissue.[6] It may be wise to incorporate a liquid *colloidal mineral formula* (found at your local nutrition store) into your regimen as well as drinking plenty of water.

Dave Palumbo.

Ted Arcidi.

indicate that 200 calories of carbohydrates will raise your insulin levels just enough to facilitate the transport of amino acids into muscle cells.[1]

UNDERSTANDING PROTEIN VALUES

The last part of the puzzle has to do with your choice of a protein that has high biological activity, meaning that it will yield the greatest amount of nitrogen. Researchers have come up with a formula that determines the protein quality of foods, called the active biological value (or BV), according to what's called the "protein digestibility corrected amino acid score," or PDCAAS.

If the availability of a food's amino acid completely matched your body's requirement, its level of protein usability would be 100 percent. Biological value, then, refers to the percentage of a food's protein usability. Proteins are also classified according to their source, such as an animal, plant, or dairy source.

PDCAAS replaces an old method of determining protein quality and nitrogen-retaining capabilities, known as protein efficiency ratio (or PER).

The PER method had involved a carefully controlled animal-feeding test, which calculated the amount of weight gained in grams for each gram of protein consumed. Casein, a milk protein, was used as a standard. PDCAAS, the method that the Food and Drug Administration currently recognizes, is based on a food's content of essential amino acids and the ratio of those aminos to each other. Scientists now have the technology to eliminate the uncertainty in determining a particular protein's ability to deposit nitrogen into muscles. Whereas the old method measured growth in relation to protein *intake* by rats, biological value (BV) involves measuring nitrogen from the dietary protein and the output of nitrogen in human feces and urine. Thus, this method focuses on how well nitrogen is *retained after* you eat a particular protein source.

Michael Francois.

Protein Principle 3   The biological value and the digestibility of a protein are critical factors in its relationship to absorption, nitrogen deposition, retention, and any subsequent muscle growth.[10]

THE ONE-MINUTE PRIMER

The next time you buy protein products, use the following guidelines to make sure you don't get a poorly formulated product—even though the source of protein is considered to have a high BV. Read the fine print, and keep an eye out for the following key words.

1. **Acid hydrolysis.** These proteins are broken down but treated with acid-on-base solutions instead of enzymes. They often have sodium contents and cause water retention.
2. **Cross-filtered ion exchange** (CFIF). This protein produces superior results

Buffy Lawrence.

Here are the current biological values of a number of proteins popularly eaten by bodybuilders:

Whey protein isolate	159
Whey protein concentrate	104
Egg white	88
Chicken	79
Casein	77

to that of protein processed through the ion-exchange method alone. CFIF removes 98 percent of denatured protein, as opposed to 90.8 percent through ion exchange.

3. **Cross-filtered ionized, or microflow, techniques.** Using these methods, no heat is required to process the protein, which preserves glutamine, the most abundant amino acid in skeletal tissue. In fact, glutamine makes up about 61 percent of the amino acid in skeletal tissue.[11]

4. **Denatured.** This occurs when protein is exposed to high temperatures—typi-

cally above 60 degrees Celsius—or to chemical agents that disrupt the bonds on which certain protein structures are based. The protein can then no longer perform its biological function.[12] Look for *undenatured* types of protein.

5. **Enzymatic hydrolysis.** This creates predigested proteins, which involves breaking them down into smaller peptides, such as di-, tri-, or oligopeptides. The peptides don't attract water into the intestine (which causes diarrhea), as single amino acids often do.

6. **Intact proteins.** These are in their original natural form and require complete digestion.

7. **Isolated amino acids.** These individual amino acids require no digestion and contain no animal by-products.

8. **Protein isolates.** These are smaller protein fragments, the same as predigested proteins.

9. **Pure crystalline aminos.** These require no digestion.

References

1. Nettl, F. 1995. *How to Do Your Protein Arithmetic.* Carson City, NV: Xipepress.

2. Gontzea, I., et al. 1974. The influence of muscular activity on nitrogen balance and on the need of protein for man. *Nutr. Rep. Int.* 10–35.

Mike Ashley.

3. Donohugh, D. L. 1983. *The Middle Years.* New York: Berkeley Books.

4. Wade, C. 1985. *Carlson Wade's Amino Acid Book.* New Canaan, CT: Keats Publishing.

5. Gershoff, S. 1990. *The Tufts University Guide to Total Nutrition.* New York: Harper and Row.

6. Marlew, G. 1994. *Electrolytes: The Spark of Life.* Murduck, FL: Nature's Publishing.

7. Sears, B. 1995. *Enter the Zone.* New York: HarperCollins Publishers.

8. Fernstrom, J., et al. 1979. Diurnal variations in plasma concentrations of tryptophan, tyrosine, and other neutral amino acids: Effects of dietary protein intake. *American Journal of Clinical Nutrition.* 32:1912–1922.

9. Anthony, J. C. 1996. Effect of meal composition on skeletal muscle protein. *Scandinavian Journal of Medicine and Science in Sports.* 6:265–272.

10. Weller, L. A., et al. 1971. Nitrogen balance of men fed amino acid mixtures based upon Rosel's requirements, egg white protein, and serum-free amino acid patterns. *Nutrition.* 205:1499–1508.

11. Lacey, J. M., and D. W. Whitemore. 1990. Is glutamine a conditionally essential amino acid? *Nutrition Reviews.* 48:297–309.

12. Starr, C., and R. Taggart. 1987. *Biology and the Unity and Diversity of Life.* 4th ed. Belmont, CA: Wadsworth Publishing.

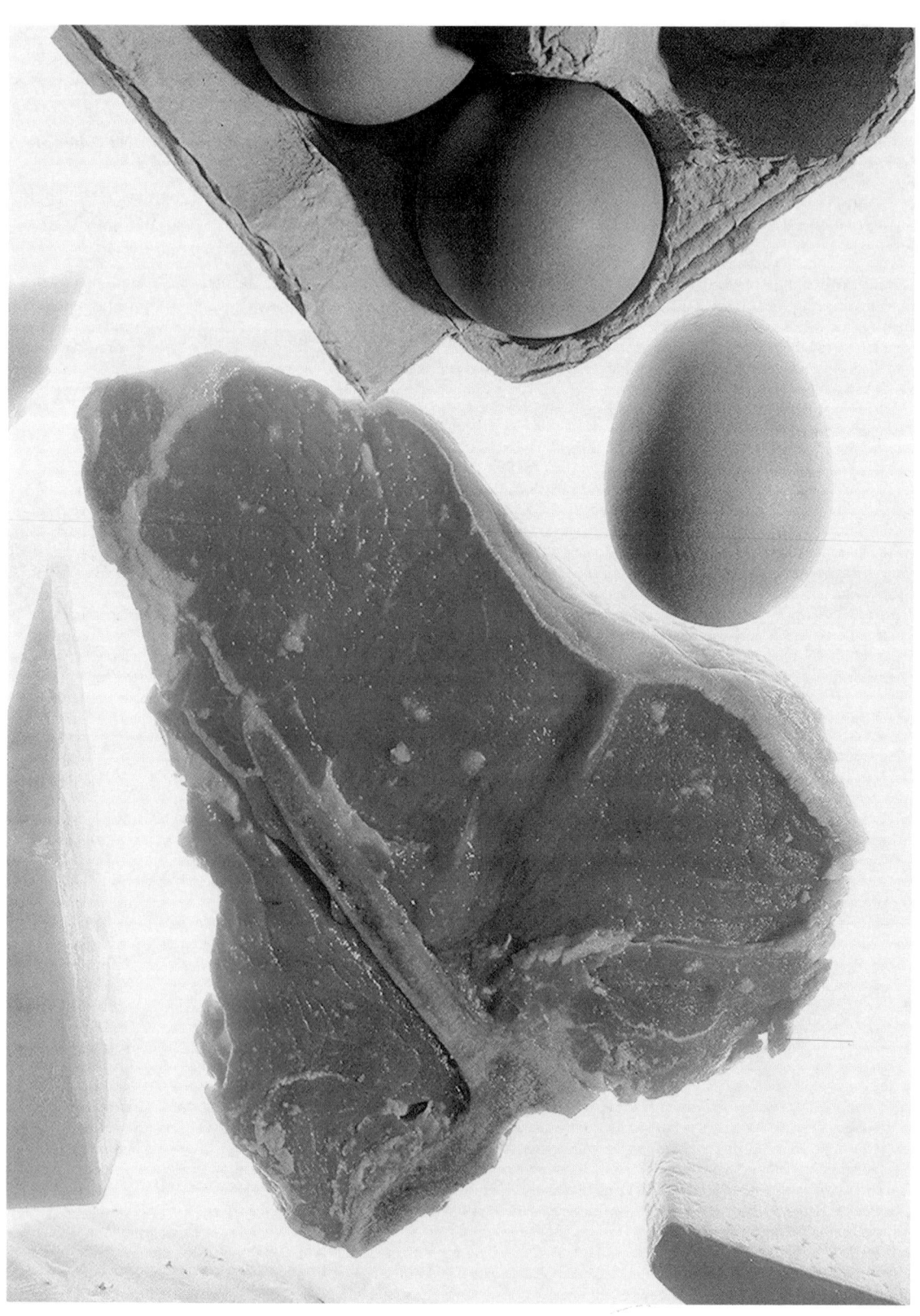

Chapter 7

DIETARY FAT: A PRIMER

BY RONALD J. ZACKER

So you think you know everything there is to know about fat? Test your knowledge with this brief pop quiz.

Which of the following statements is correct?

a. Fats can make you fat.
b. Fats can make you lean.
c. Fats can boost your immune system.
d. Fats can suppress your immune system.
e. Fats can promote heart disease.
f. Fats can prevent heart disease.
g. Fats are good.
h. Fats are bad.
i. All of the above.

Believe it or not, in the right context all of these statements are true. Are you confused? It's no wonder. Fat is a favorite topic in the media, with new information emerging almost weekly. Unfortunately, the information is often contradictory, and the sheer volume of nutrition-based facts and figures can easily become overwhelming. My purpose here is to clear up much of the confusion about fat and show you how to adjust your fat intake to achieve optimum levels of health, vitality, and performance.

Let's begin by examining the different types of fat you most likely encounter in your diet.

CHOLESTEROL

Sources include animal-based foods such as egg yolks, milk, red meat, fish, shellfish, poultry, organ meats, and butter. Cholesterol is an essential metabolite in animal cells, and it performs several important functions in the body. It plays a role as a structural component of cell membranes and a precursor for the synthesis of steroid hormones, such as testosterone. Cholesterol is not, however, an essential nutrient, meaning that it can be synthesized in the body and you don't have to get it from your diet.

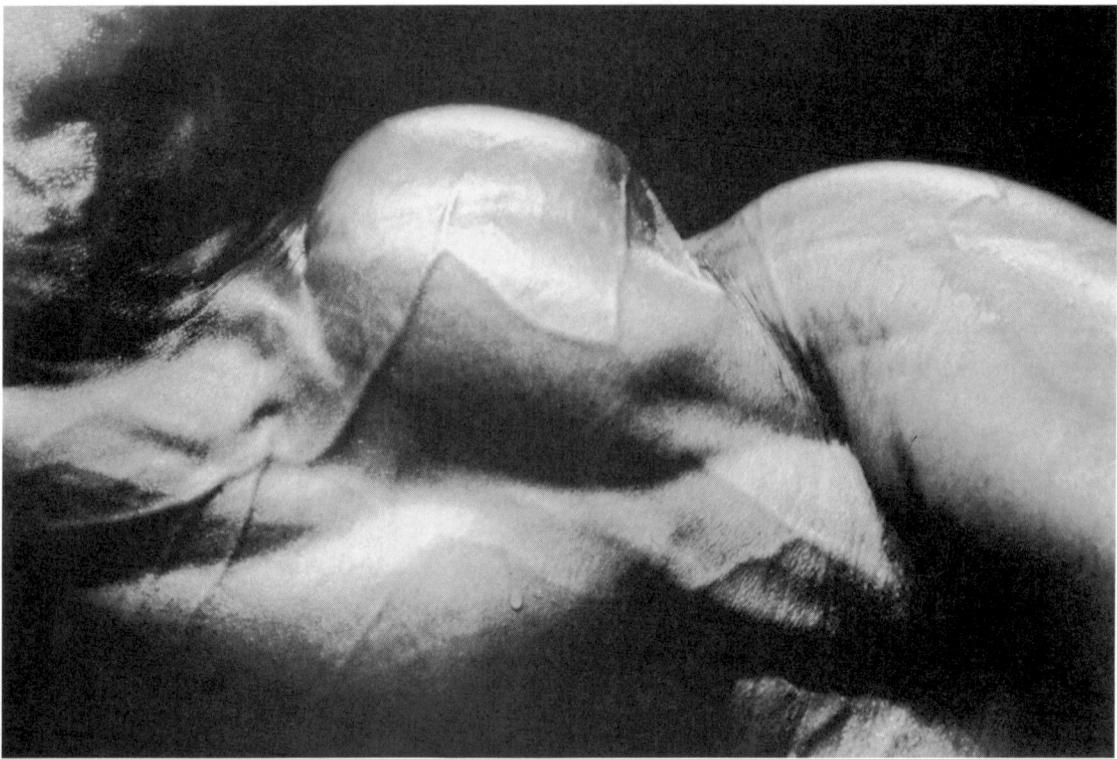

Too much cholesterol in your blood, a condition known as *hypercholesterolemia*, is a risk factor for heart disease. This is true especially if you have a particularly high ratio of low-density lipoproteins, also known as bad cholesterol, to high-density lipoproteins, or good cholesterol. You can control this ratio to some degree. For instance, exercise raises HDLs, while diet composition, body composition, and eating patterns can influence LDLs. Cigarette smoking is detrimental with both types of cholesterol, so whatever you do, quit smoking!

Since you don't need to take in cholesterol (because your body makes it) and too much cholesterol is a risk factor for heart disease, the question is, Do you need to worry about the cholesterol content of your food? As it turns out, even if you were concerned about heart disease, only 10 to 25 percent of people can lower their LDLs simply by eating less cholesterol-containing food. For most people

Kevin Hall.

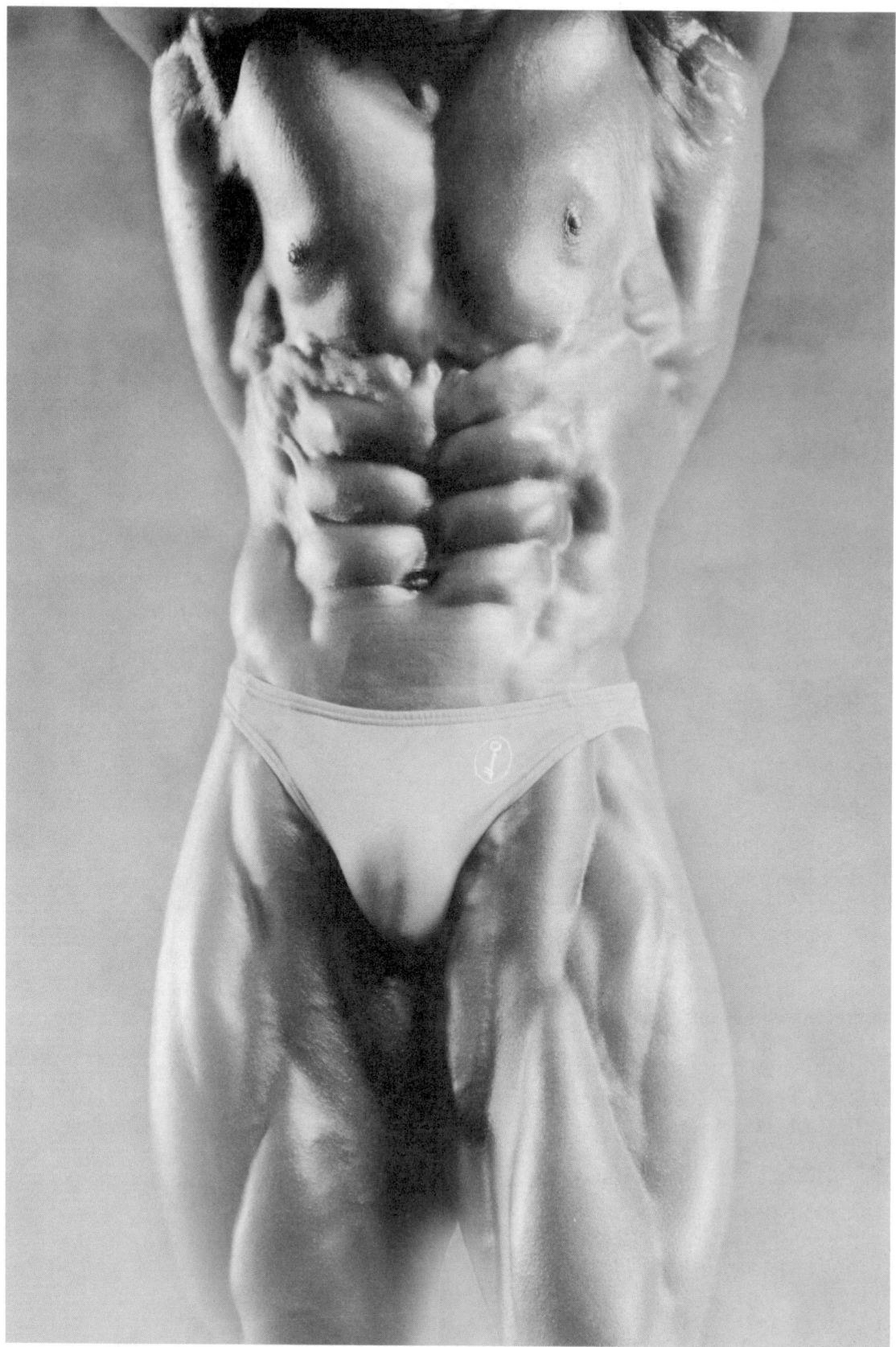

Thierry Pastel.

Cory Everson.

Jonathan Lawson.

it's the amount of *saturated fat* in the diet that has the greatest influence on cholesterol levels. So the bottom line on cholesterol is, unless you eat a lot of organ meats—like brains—you don't really need to worry about the cholesterol content of your food.

SATURATED FATS, OR SATURATED FATTY ACIDS (SFAs)

Sources include the same foods that contain cholesterol, as well as palm, coconut, and hydrogenated oils such as margarine (see "Hydrogenated Fats"). The body needs very little saturated fat. Too much of any fat can raise your blood lipid, or fat, levels and increase your risk of heart disease. Too much saturated fat can also raise LDL cholesterol

levels, further increasing your risk. What's more, it can impair certain aspects of your immune system.

The best course of action, then, is to avoid fatty animal products like egg yolks; whole milk; butter; fatty cuts of meat and poultry; and palm, coconut, and hydrogenated oils. This will also reduce your consumption of cholesterol (in case you were still concerned about that).

You say you already know all of the above? Then let's get into some more intriguing fats.

OTHER FATS

Polyunsaturated fats, or polyunsaturated fatty acids (PUFAs)

You know saturated fats are bad. You may also have heard that PUFAS are the essential fatty acids, meaning you must get them from your diet because your body cannot make them. Who cares? you say. Everyone, including McDonald's, is now using the so-called heart-healthy polyunsaturated fats like vegetable oil. Well, there are two kinds of PUFAS, and you need to consider how both of them fit into the big picture.

Linoleic Acid Also called omega-6, or n-6, fatty acids. Sources of linoleic acid include most vegetable oils (such as corn, safflower, sunflower, and soybean oils) and all the foods made with those oils, as well as walnuts.

Jean-Pierre Fux.

Rich Piana.

Linolenic Acid Also called omega-3, or n-3, fatty acids. Sources of linolenic acid include fatty, cold-water fish and their oils, flaxseed oil, and, to a much lesser extent, soybean and canola oils.

Omega-6 fatty acids are indeed essential nutrients, and they're found in abundance in the foods you frequently encounter. That's terrific. The problem is that they may be a little *too easy* to get from your diet, relative to omega-3 fatty acids. In nature it's always important to maintain a *balance*. It seems that the ratio of omega-6 to omega-3 fatty acids in the diet is what influences eicosanoids production, which in turn influences immune function and heart disease risk.

If you're at all familiar with *The Zone* by Barry Sears, you may have already heard of eicosanoids. They're hormonelike compounds synthesized from both omega-6 and omega-3 polyunsaturated fatty acids. These hormonelike

Jean-Pierre Fux.

omega-6 and omega-3 fatty acids for ideal eicosanoid production. Just what this ideal ratio should be is still largely disputed; however, Canada, the only national government to establish guidelines for PUFA consumption, suggests that this ratio of omega-6 to omega-3 fatty acids should be about 4 to 1. The typical American diet is closer to 10 to 1.

Chances are you're already getting enough omega-6 fats in your diet, and it would be very difficult to eat enough omega-3 fats to upset the balance in the other direction. So you probably need to seek out more foods rich in omega-3 fats to keep your eicosanoid production balanced. Once you achieve that, you should experience improved immune function—which is especially important for bodybuilders and athletes—and a lowered risk of heart disease. Fish appear to be the most reliable sources of omega-3 fats. If you cannot consume enough omega-3s from fish, you may need to consider supplements like fish-oil capsules or flaxseed oil.

compounds, of which there are four (prostaglandins, prostacyclins, thromboxanes, and leukotrienes), are important and potent regulators of body functions such as blood pressure, blood clotting, and immune or inflammatory responses. Just how potent they are is still up for debate. Nevertheless, a relationship clearly does exist.

I'll spare you the biochemical details of how that works, but too much omega-6 fat relative to omega-3 fat in the diet can produce more so-called bad eicosanoids relative to good ones.

You already know that too much of any fat can increase your risk of heart disease. Too much omega-6 can also suppress the immune system, producing an excess of bad eicosanoids. These eicosanoids are inflammatory and promote platelet aggregation, which clogs arteries, further increasing your risk of heart disease. Does that mean you should omit omega-6 fats from your diet? Absolutely not. Remember, the idea is to get a balance of

Craig Titus.

Craig Titus.

Monounsaturated fats, or mono-unsaturated fatty acids (MUFAs)

Sources include olive oil, avocados, and, to a lesser extent, canola, sesame, and peanut oils, as well as almonds and pecans. MUFAs are considered to be neutral fats. They don't affect the ratio of omega-6 to omega-3, so they don't influence eicosanoid production or the related regulatory function. Like polyunsaturated fats, monounsaturated fats don't increase LDL cholesterol in the blood, which is a good thing. What's more, unlike most other fats, MUFAs have been shown to maintain HDL blood cholesterol levels when used as part of a diet to reduce total fat. To put that another way, normally when the total fat content of the diet is reduced, blood concentrations of both LDL and HDL cholesterol are also reduced. Ideally, the goal is to reduce LDLs while maintaining or raising HDLs. When MUFAs replace other fats in an overall fat-reduced diet, this ideal phenomenon is thought to occur.

So once you consume your essential polyunsaturated fatty acids—in a somewhat balanced ratio, of course—monounsaturated fatty acids would be the preferred choice for any additional fat you consume.

Before you get any funny ideas about breaking out the shot glasses for some olive oil kamikazes, you must remember that too much of any fat can increase your blood lipids, at least temporarily, and may therefore increase your risk of heart disease. Of course, this is of greatest concern to those who have an existing heart condition. Also keep in mind that MUFAs, like most fats, contain nine calories per gram, which can add up quickly and make you fat if you're not careful.

Hydrogenated fats

Technically speaking, hydrogenated fats are not saturated fats. They're unsaturated fats that have had hydrogen added to them to varying degrees—hence the name. For instance, liquid margarine that comes in squeeze containers is less hydrogenated than hard, stick margarine. The hydrogenation process essentially makes the fats behave like saturated fats in your body, which isn't good. So try to avoid foods containing hydrogenated fats—or at least pick ones that have a low degree of hydrogenation, such as liquid margarine. Another common substitution would be to choose so-called natural peanut butter, the kind you have to refrigerate, over Skippy or Jif (products that contain hydrogenated oil). Remember to always read the label.

Fake Fats   These include Oatrim, Z-Trim, microparticulated protein, Salatrim, and Olestra. These so-called fat replacers can be made of carbohydrate, protein, or fat. They're usually found in snack foods, desserts, and other things you shouldn't be eating a lot of anyway. They were designed to mimic the flavors and textures of fat-based foods, only with fewer calories—and they do. The question is, Have you ever eaten a reduced-fat

Darrem Charles.

Terry Mitsos.

product that was every bit as satisfying as the original? Some come close, but fat is a difficult ingredient to replace.

The most recent fat substitute to come on the market, Olestra, may be the exception. Because it is a fat, albeit a man-made one, Olestra should provide all of the desirable characteristics associated with fat. What's more, because Olestra is purposefully designed to not be absorbed in your intestine, you won't get any energy—that is, calories—from it. It sounds pretty terrific so far, doesn't it?

The only problem is that when fat isn't absorbed, it ends up in the stool. The medical term for this is *steatorrhea*, and it's usually accompanied by an oily, particularly foul case of diarrhea. In more severe cases fat malabsorption may lead to a general malabsorption of other nutrients, particularly the fat-soluble vitamins. So how good does Olestra sound now?

Because this product is still in the experimental stage, we'll just have to wait and see if it pans out or not. Until then I believe that, heart condition notwithstanding, if you're

going to eat fatty junk foods, eat the real thing to stop your craving. Just be sure to use moderation when you do, and try not to make a habit of eating nutrient-sparse, high-fat foods.

Skip La Cour.

Conjugated Linoleic Acids (CLAs)

Sources include animal foods like milk and meat, as well as supplement capsules. One reputable supplement company claims that CLA is a potent antioxidant, an anabolic growth factor, a fat-burning agent, a cancer-preventing agent, and an immune-system booster. Whew! Where can I get some?

All of those claims were based on legitimate scientific studies that were conducted to determine the various effects of CLA supplementation in animals. The results of the studies do show that CLA may have great potential applications for humans. Be that as it may, we don't yet know enough about the effects of CLA supplementation on humans to recommend its use. And because its cost is relatively high, I'd rather see people spend the money on nutritious food.

THE BOTTOM LINE FOR FATS

Most people really don't need to be too concerned about cholesterol intake, and everyone should try to limit saturated fat in his or her diet by consuming fewer fatty animal products. People should also try to balance their consumption of omega-3 and omega-6 polyunsaturated fats by eating more fish or taking an omega-3 supplement and by substituting canola and soybean oils for corn oil. Finally, folks should continue to enjoy omega-6 and monounsaturated fats in moderation.

You may now be wondering just how much fat you should eat. In other words, what percentage of your diet should consist of fat. Now, that's a topic worthy of its own article, don't you think?

Chapter 8

ANOTHER LOOK AT THE ANABOLIC DIET

BY JUDD BIASIOTTO, PH.D.

What if I told you that you could get massively muscular and shredded to the bone by eating a lot of foods you've been told are bad for you? Think about steaks, chops, omelets—even pizza—and if that doesn't have you drooling, think about what you'll look like when you're as big and ripped as you can be.

Maybe you have heard about body-builders having success with a high-fat, high-protein regimen and you didn't believe it. "Eat fatty foods to get lean?" you say doubtfully. "That goes against everything I know about nutrition."

Well, you can believe it, folks. The new high-protein, high-fat diet really works. Thanks to modern nutritional science the impossible becomes the possible, so read on to find out how you, too, can eat your way to the body of your dreams—while you're busting your butt in the gym, of course.

A SIMPLE TWO-PHASE SYSTEM

This new diet is similar to Mauro Di Pasquale's *Anabolic Diet* and to the plan described by Dan Duchaine in his book *Body Opus*. It consists of two distinct phases: carbo-hydrate depletion and carbohydrate loading. Basically, you cut carbs for 5 days during the week, load for 2 days on the weekend, and then repeat the 7-day cycle ad infinitum.

Let's start with phase 1, 5 days of carbohy-drate depletion, in which your goal is to take in zero carbohydrates, with 55 to 75 percent of your calories coming from fat and 25 to 45 percent coming from protein.

"Seventy-five percent fat—are you nuts?" you scream. Absolutely not, and what's more, you can have all the delicious, formerly forbid-den foods you crave and not get fat. Here's an idea of how it works.

you'll be eating so many things you love that you won't miss the foods you're giving up.

This rule is based on something else you may not believe: humans get fat only when they mix fat and carbs together. When you eat the two food groups together, the carbs are used for energy and the fat is stored as—you guessed it—bodyfat. But when you deprive the body of carbs, it starts burning fat.

"Don't I need carbohydrates for energy?" you protest. Doesn't the brain need glucose for energy? The answer to both questions is no. During ketosis your body simply switches to using dietary fat and bodyfat for energy. Look at the Eskimos. They've been carb-depleting for ages, yet they live very healthy, long lives with only rare cases of heart disease.

"But won't I get arteriosclerosis?" Again the answer is a resounding no. Believe it or not, ketosis reduces cholesterol levels because you force the body to live on fatty acids and cholesterol.

Now, a diet works only as long as it's satisfying and filling. Since dietary fat is far more satiating than carbohydrates, during phase 1 you won't have to worry about those tremendous hunger pangs that always strike when you're on a high-carb, low-calorie, and low-fat diet. In fact, one of the major drawbacks to those eating plans is the fact that the meals are usually digested in about a half hour. The

When you stop eating carbohydrates, your body goes into a metabolic state called *ketosis*, in which it's forced to switch over to an alternative fuel source for energy. Since you're also inundating it with dietary fat, it switches from burning carbs for energy to burning ingested fat and, most important, *stored* bodyfat. So by causing your body to go into ketosis, you turn it into a fat-burning machine, and as long as you keep your carbs to a minimum and stay in a state of ketosis, you won't get fat.

Now you're probably wondering, "What's the catch? This is too good to be true." The only catch is that you must keep carbohydrate intake to an absolute minimum during the 5 days of phase 1. Sticking to that minimum shouldn't be too difficult, however, because

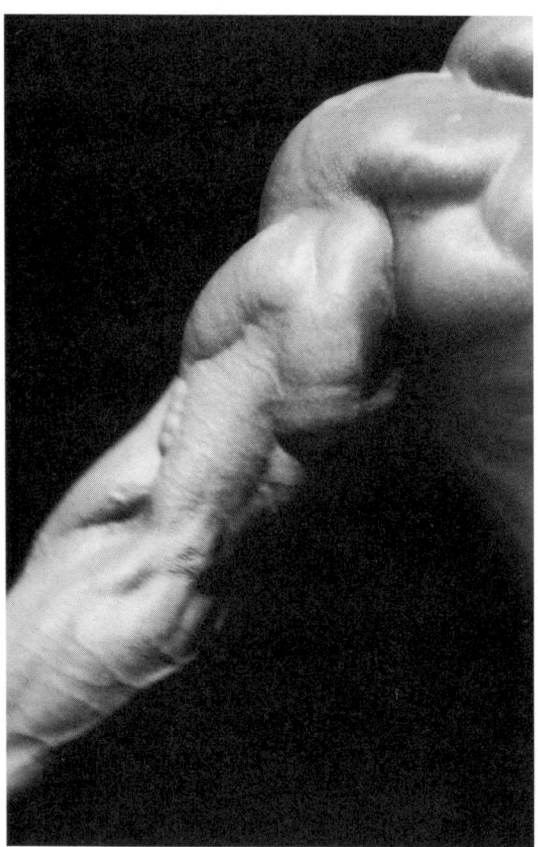

usual scenario is excruciating hunger pangs leading to binge eating—leading to dieters giving up altogether.

With high-fat plus low-carb meals composed primarily of meat, eggs, and cheese, you slow down the digestion process considerably. You won't be continually thinking about food the way you do on those high-carb and low-fat diets. Furthermore, high-carb meals typically cause your body to secrete insulin, which in turn causes the hunger pangs described above. Because dietary fat blunts the secretion of insulin, the lack of fat in the diet magnifies the insulin secretion caused by the carbs. Anyone who's experienced insatiable hunger while eating chocolate bars will know what I'm talking about: you eat one and you just can't seem to quit pigging out on sugary foods. That won't happen on this diet—specifically, as I mentioned before, because dietary fat blunts the secretion of insulin. Remember, if you stay in ketosis, you're guaranteed to stay lean.

When you follow this diet, it's absolutely mandatory that you keep a food diary and

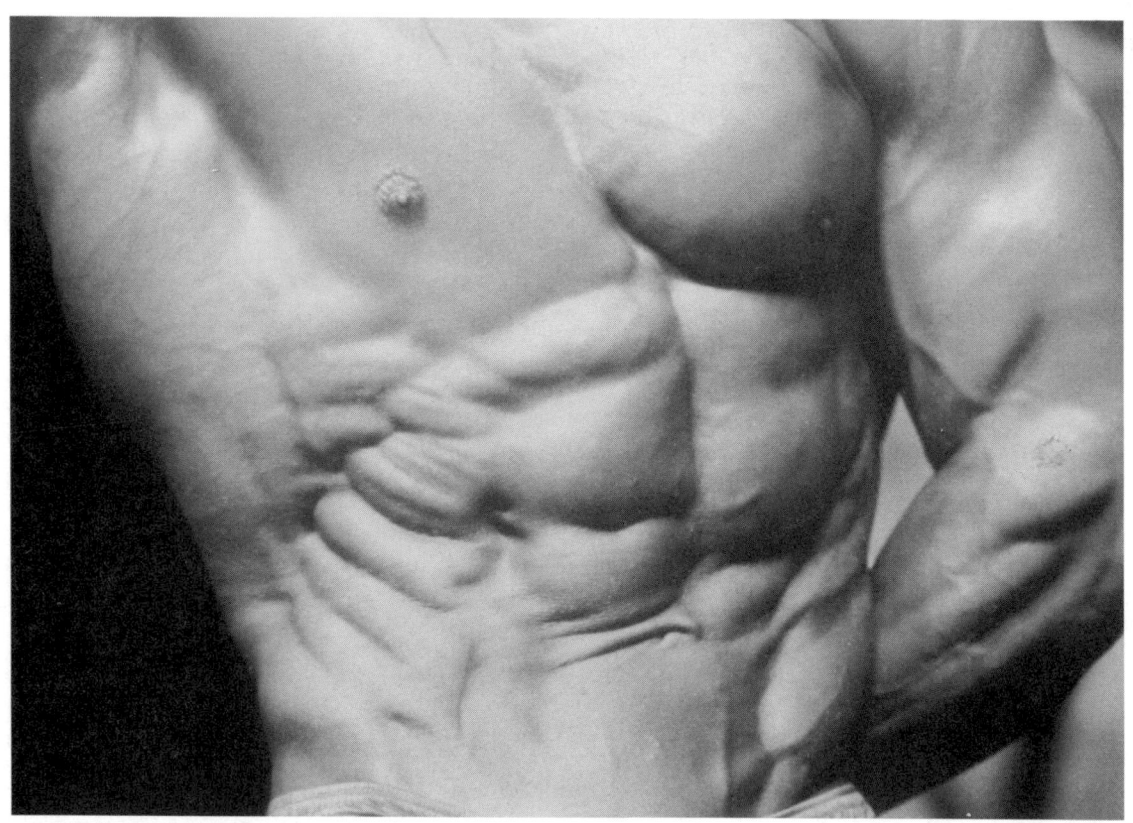

Jean-Pierre Fux.

Mike Quinn.

record your exact intake of protein, fat, carbo-hydrates, and calories each day. Getting down to zero carbs is not a realistic goal. As long as you keep your carbs below 30 grams, or 120 calories, a day and your total dietary fat to a minimum of 55 percent of calories, you should remain in ketosis. That amount should make the diet fairly palatable, as you'll be able to have a little steak sauce or even have a beer or two at night if you've diligently avoided carbs all day.

As noted, the goal of phase 1 is to carb-deplete—to empty the muscle cells of glycogen and to force the body to burn fat through ketosis. After 5 days of that regimen you switch to phase 2, the carbohydrate-loading phase. The goal here is to cram carbs into the muscle by eating a lot of them. You may have heard about marathon runners using carb loading to increase endurance or bodybuilders using it to temporarily increase size dramatically just before a contest. Phase 1, then, is the cutting phase, and phase 2 could be considered the growth, or bulking, phase.

During the carbohydrate-loading phase the goal is to ingest roughly 60 percent carbs, 20 percent protein, and 20 percent fat. The two days become a virtual pigfest, during which pretty much anything is fair game to eat—Burger King sandwiches, McDonald's fries, Dairy Queen banana splits, all the Dunkin' Donuts holes you want, pizza, chocolate, soda pop, and even sugar sandwiches! The wonderful thing about this diet is that for those two days you can satisfy all your cravings for your favorite foods. Granted, you do have to be fairly selective during the week in order to achieve ketosis, and you may find yourself becoming antsy. Come the weekend,

Michael Francois.

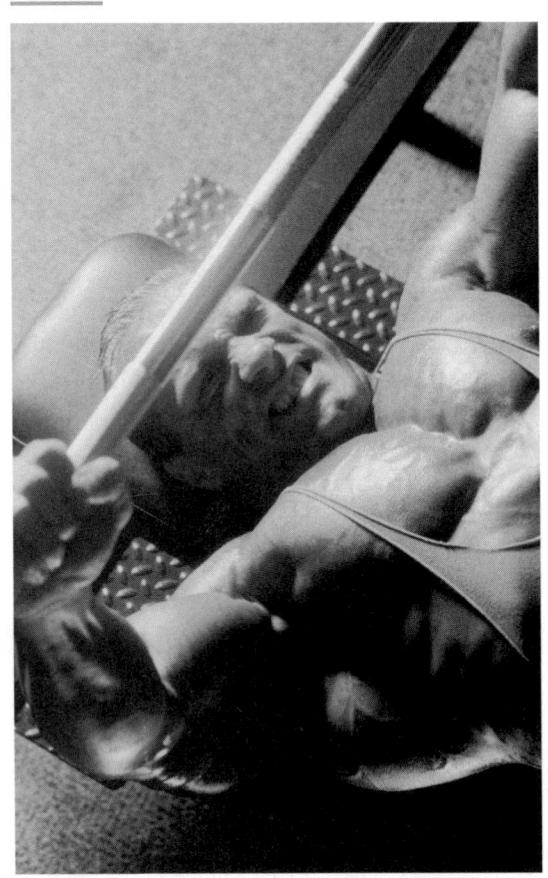

Katy Rickman.

however, you can truly go wild and not feel guilty. Be sure to curtail the carb loading after 48 hours though! You don't want any problems with insulin. Yes, I know it's an anabolic hormone, but it can cause fat storage when secreted in excess. Some bodybuilders may have to limit the carb loading to fewer than 48 hours. Experiment and find your own metabolic limit. When you look in the mirror and see that you're smoothing out, stop carb loading and go back to ketosis. If you carb-load correctly, your muscles should be fuller, rounder, and pumped to the max. If you overdo it, you'll start smoothing out and laying on the fat. As I said, experiment so that you can time your carb loading perfectly.

HOW THE HIGH-FAT/LOW-CARB DIET WORKS

You don't have to know everything about nutrition to use this diet. If you grasp the basics and follow the guidelines outlined above, you're going to get big and ripped. It's not critical that you understand why the diet works, but in case you're interested—or planning to be on *Jeopardy*—here's a rundown of the processes that come into play. The fact is, the better you understand the diet, the more motivated you'll be to use it.

During phase 1, as you carb-deplete, your pancreas stops secreting insulin and instead starts to secrete a hormone that has the exact opposite effect, glucagon. Although insulin is a powerful anabolic hormone, it's also fat producing. That explains why people with type 2 diabetes—people whose pancreas secretes

Jodi Friedman.

Brandy Hale.

abnormal, excessive amounts of insulin due to impaired insulin receptor sensitivity—are usually more muscular but also fatter than people who have other forms of diabetes.

Insulin also retards the release of human growth hormone (HGH). As many of you are aware, HGH is one of the body's more powerful anabolic and lipolytic—that is, fat-burning—hormones. Consequently, by eating a high-carb diet, which increases the secretion of insulin, you actually work to inhibit fat loss and muscle-mass acquisition. On the other hand, glucagon is a very powerful lipolytic hormone that also coaxes the body to produce more HGH. You may have heard of professional bodybuilders using glucagon injections to accelerate fat loss and increase HGH secretion, a dangerous practice. The question is, Can you increase glucagon secretion to accelerate fat loss and increase HGH secretion without resorting to potentially dangerous injections? The answer is yes, and it lies in ketosis.

As you carb-deplete, your blood glucose levels plummet, and when they dip below a certain point, the pancreas starts secreting glucagon—and that means more HGH and more bodyfat utilization, which translates into more lean muscle mass.

It gets even better because your body also starts producing more testosterone. During the five days that you consume a lot of cholesterol from all the animal-protein foods, your body will secrete optimal amounts of testosterone. Why? Because cholesterol, fat, and red meat are important precursors to testosterone production. Testosterone and cholesterol have nearly identical chemical structures, and so there seems to be a high relationship between testosterone production and fat consumption. True vegans—that is, people who eschew all animal products—make poor athletes. A current theory is that this may be due to impaired

testosterone production caused by inadequate intakes of cholesterol, fat, and red meat.

As for why you get so lean, understand that on conventional low-fat plus high-carb diets all of the lipolytic, fat-burning enzymes shut down while all the lipogenic, or fat-producing, ones rev up as the body tries to store bodyfat to safeguard against famine. Essentially, your body becomes adept at getting fat. On a high-fat plus low-carb diet the opposite phenomenon occurs. All of the fat-burning enzymes rev back up, while the fat-producing ones start to shut down. As amazing as it seems, by eating more fat, you help your body become less fat.

Many critics of high-fat ketosis diets argue that carbohydrates are crucial to bodybuilders because of their protein-sparing, or anticatabolic, effect. Specifically, carbs inhibit muscle breakdown because the body uses them for energy instead of cannibalizing muscle tissue. Although that's true, it's also true that fats have an even greater anticatabolic, muscle-sparing effect. Research has consistently proved that humans eating high-fat diets lose much less muscle mass than those consuming high-carb diets when injected with corticosteroids, which are medications that destroy or catabolize muscle tissue. As athletes train, there's an ongoing war between the anabolic and catabolic hormones released during exercise. The goal in athletics is to tip the scales in favor of the anabolic hormones while downplaying the effects of the catabolic ones.

The main catabolic hormone that robs many bodybuilders of progress is *cortisol*. High levels of cortisol directly impede the production of testosterone in the testicles. In addition, all the factors that encourage growth hormone release are depressed by cortisol. Obviously, the lower the cortisol level, the better it is for the athlete. Although it's impossible for the body to remain cortisol free, you can control its effect fairly well with proper nutrition and rest. As previously indicated, a high-fat diet inhibits the muscle-destroying effects of cortisol and keeps the body in an anabolic state. [*Note:* Supplements such as Champion Nutrition's Cortistat and Muscle-Link's Cort-Bloc, which contain phosphatidyl-serine, can also suppress cortisol and its catabolic effects.]

With conventional carbohydrate-based diets, insulin is released after carb ingestion and the carbs are converted into glucose, which fuels the body. During ketosis, since carbs aren't available, glucagon is released instead of insulin, and dietary fats are converted into ketones. Ketones then take over all of glucose's functions—with one important distinction: while excess glucose over and above metabolic requirements can and will be stored as bodyfat, excess ketones are simply excreted in the urine. In other words, in the absence of carbohydrates it's metabolically impossible for the body to store ingested dietary fat as bodyfat.

Now let's talk about the hormonal cascade that occurs on the weekends, during phase 2. During the week insulin secretion is curtailed, while insulin receptor sites in the body increase their sensitivity. Come the weekend, as you reverse gears from carb depletion to carb loading, your pancreas quits secreting glucagon and starts secreting tremendous amounts of insulin. Because of the body's increased insulin sensitivity, compounded by its hypersecretion of insulin, a phenomenon known as carbohydrate loading occurs in the muscles. They become engorged with glycogen, water, and nutrients. Bodybuilders carb-load before a contest because of its obvious cosmetic effects—dramatic muscle fullness and roundness. Powerlifters and long-distance runners do it before a meet because of the athletic advantages it offers—increased muscular strength and endurance due to the muscles being supersaturated with glycogen, water, and nutrient substances.

In addition, there's a growth effect from the continual depleting and supersaturating of glycogen in the muscles, week in and week out, on this diet. You may have heard bodybuilders swear they put on the most mass *after* they compete. That occurs because they depleted their bodies of nutrients for weeks to get shredded; then after the show, as they pigged out and made up for the dietary deprivation, their bodies overcompensated, became flooded with nutrients, and switched gears from a catabolic, precontest diet state to an anabolic, off-season bulking state. Most bodybuilders compete in only one contest a year. Using this diet is like competing every week. Think of the growth you could achieve by duplicating this depletion and overcompensation cycle a number of times throughout the year.

On the weekends your bulking phase will be enhanced by your greatly increased appetite. As you carb-load on the weekend, you may experience the hypoglycemic-induced hunger pangs you didn't have during your depletion days. Consequently, you won't have to worry about trying to eat enough high-carb foods to trigger the carbohydrate-loading effect. What's more, since high-carb foods are digested faster than high-fat foods, you may find that on the weekends you can eat twice as many meals per day as you can during the week. Carb loading will be easier than you may have thought.

If that's not enough to convince you to try this diet, let's talk about the most powerful ergogenic known to man: insulin-like growth factor 1, or IGF-1. Scientists now know that IGF-1 is the anabolic hormone responsible for building muscle mass in humans; however, at current prices it would cost a bodybuilder thousands of dollars a day to use the dosages that were used in the research. Professional bodybuilders have found another way to flood the body with IGF-1, namely, by using a combination of HGH, testosterone, and insulin injections. Research has indicated that nearly all of the growth effects of HGH come not from the growth hormone itself but from its ability to coax the liver into producing more IGF-1. Bodybuilders then add testosterone to this pharmaceutical cocktail because HGH needs an androgenic environment in which to exert its fullest anabolic effect. The insulin is used also because it considerably increases the half-life of IGF-1 from only a few minutes to 16 hours.

Insulin also magnifies the anabolic potential of testosterone by decreasing levels of globulin, a protein that binds to testosterone, keeping it from exhibiting its anabolic properties. Only the free form of testosterone is metabolically active. When you're on this diet, HGH (and thus IGF-1) and testosterone levels are elevated through the 5 weekdays of ketosis. Then, as you switch from carb depleting to carb loading, your body senses the drastic change as a metabolic shock, releasing even more testosterone and HGH, and even more IGF-1, in addition to the hypersecretion of insulin.

So by using the diet, you coax your body into replicating the most powerful hormonal stack used by today's pro bodybuilders. No wonder it triggers such extreme muscle mass acquisition and bizarre fat loss.

Now, don't get your hopes up too high. Although the diet ensures maximal production of those crucial muscle-building hormones, you won't replicate the dramatic results achieved by bodybuilders who resort to *injecting* the above compounds. On the other hand, you won't suffer any of the dramatic *side effects* of those medications. I believe that this diet is a genuine steroid alternative. By coaxing the body's own internal muscle-building hormones maximally through dietary manipulation, you progress far beyond what you could achieve with conventional high-carb plus low-fat diets—without having to play a pharmaceutical game of Russian roulette.

Lee Apperson.

Chapter 9

ACETYL-L-CARNITINE: STATE-OF-THE-ART SUPPLEMENT

BY GREG ZULAK

Bodybuilding supplements have come a long way in the past 50 years. Whereas state-of-the-art used to mean soybean protein powder, desiccated liver tablets, wheat germ oil, and amino acid capsules, in recent years such exotic-sounding substances as creatine monohydrate, hydroxymethylbutyrate (HMB), conjugated linoleic acid (CLA), dehydroepiandrosterone (DHEA), glutamine, and ion-exchanged whey protein have dominated the scene. Now we have acetyl-L-carnitine, or ALC, a supplement that definitely seems to have powerful muscle-building effects for bodybuilders and strength and fitness athletes. Before we get into what the stuff is and how it works, however, it's important to understand the role of testosterone in building muscle.

TESTOSTERONE AND MUSCLE BUILDING

The number-one factor relating to muscle growth and strength increases in males is the hormone testosterone. The more you have, the easier it is to build muscle. (This is one reason that women have difficulty building muscle—they have naturally low testosterone levels and high estrogen levels.) Testosterone is the hormone responsible for male characteristics. It signals the body to increase protein synthesis in muscles as well as to enhance creatine phosphate synthesis.

Bodybuilders and other athletes who use anabolic steroids and synthetic testosterone drugs are familiar with the effects of the increased production of those two vital muscle-building components. Unfortunately, steroids and synthetic testosterone also have negative side effects. Some athletes take them anyway, but a vast number are wary of such drugs and are looking for alternative ways of increasing testosterone naturally. ALC is such an alternative. To put it succinctly, anything that raises testosterone levels dramatically increases a bodybuilder's muscle mass, strength, and recovery ability—and this new supplement fills the bill.

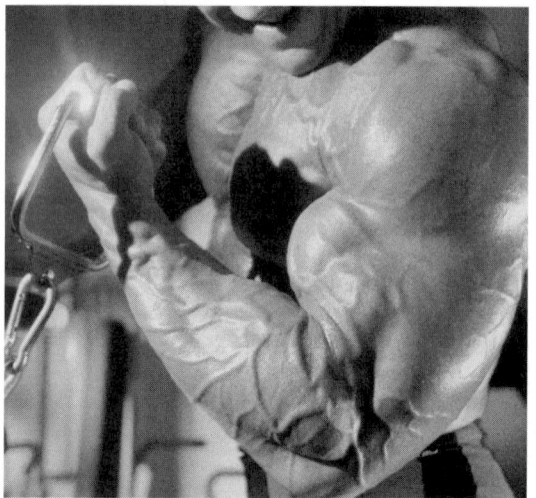

Lee Labrada.

WHAT THE EXPERTS SAY ABOUT ALC

Mauro Di Pasquale, M.D., and Paul G. Newman of the Canadian research company MuscleTech were the first to tell me of the benefits of acetyl-L-carnitine. Both men were very enthusiastic about the nutrient's muscle-building potential, and shortly after talking with them, I spoke with several bodybuilders who were using a supplement called Acetabolan that contained ALC, including Greg Kovacs, the biggest and strongest bodybuilder in the world. (He weighs a solid 390 pounds in the off-season and has 24-inch arms, a 68-inch chest, and 35-inch thighs; he incline-presses

Craig Titus.

Jennifer Goodwin.

Karl List and Jodi Friedman.

As nutritionally savvy bodybuilders are aware, anything that increases testosterone while reducing the catabolic effects of cortisol is going to help build more lean mass.

"A supplement that increases testosterone levels is acetyl-L-carnitine. Not L-carnitine, but acetyl-L-carnitine," Colman explained in a recent article. "The mechanism is unclear at the moment but probably involves the unique stimulating effects of ALC on acetylcholine neurotransmission in the striatal cortex of your brain.

"Once it gets into the brain, ALC performs miracles," Colgan continued. "You would expect that it also acts as an anticatabolic. Why? Because when the neurotransmitters in the striatal cortex are working well, they help

700 pounds for reps and can perform behind-the-neck presses with 455 pounds for 8 reps.) All reported significant gains in new lean muscle mass, strength, and recovery.

Good word of mouth is the best indication that a product truly works well. It's one thing to see a magazine ad that hypes a product like crazy (remember all the hoopla over Similax and dibencozide?), but when people at the gym are raving about their gains, you know it's something worthwhile.

Acetyl-L-carnitine is the acetylated ester of the amino acid L-carnitine. In its acetylated form it can easily pass through the blood-brain barrier. Nutritional expert Michael Colgan, M.D. and director of the San Diego–based Colgan Institute of Nutritional Science for nearly 20 years, has helped develop some of the most effective food supplements. He has praised ALC highly both in *Muscular Development* magazine and in his latest book, *Hormonal Health*. The supplement has important qualities relating to testosterone and cortisol levels in the body, according to Colgan.

Sandy Riddell.

Jean-Pierre Fux.

to keep cortisol under control. Cortisol, commonly known as the stress hormone, is highly catabolic to muscle. [There have been] no human studies yet, but animal studies do show greatly reduced cortisol levels in animals subjected to stress when they are supplemented with ALC. It is a good bet it will work in humans in the same way."

Due to the substance's powerful effects, "Pharmaceutical companies who realize ALC's potential have already petitioned the FDA to restrict it," Colgan stated. If this were to happen, it would be a major blow to natural bodybuilders, who don't want to use anabolic steroids or other anticatabolic drugs such as clenbuterol, human growth hormone, insulin, and IGF-1.

Di Pasquale, a former world champion powerlifter and one of the world's most recognized experts on both drugs and nutrition in sports—as well as the developer of the high-fat anabolic diet—is another authority who recommends ALC. Citing its ability to stimulate testosterone production and its protective

effect on selected body tissues, including skeletal muscle, he gave it the highest rating in his book *Bodybuilding Supplement Review*.

Another expert who thinks ALC is one of the most effective supplements a bodybuilder or strength athlete can take is Charles Poliquin, strength coach for Canada's Olympic skiers, bobsledders, cyclists, track-and-field athletes, and weight lifters. Poliquin also trains many national-level and world-class powerlifters, is

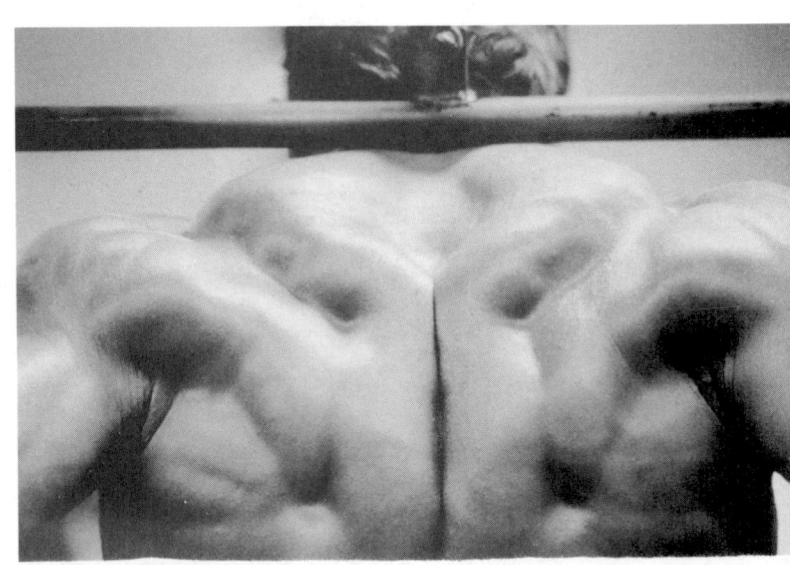

a strength consultant to the Chicago Bulls and several other professional football and basketball teams, and is a personal trainer to Prince Albert of Monaco. Since Poliquin travels to Europe every month, he knows many of the continent's top coaches, trainers, and athletes in various sports, and he reports that ALC is very popular among his colleagues there.

"ALC reportedly offers the following benefits to bodybuilders," Poliquin said in a recent article. "[It] may prevent stress-related reductions in testosterone levels; may boost energy metabolism at the cellular level; may improve the sensitivity of receptors that trigger and mediate acetylcholine release; may help maintain nerve growth factor. I've found that it significantly improves mental focus in training."

Monica Brant.

WHERE TO GET ALC

At this time the supplement isn't available in most health-food stores. A few select companies are producing small quantities of it. The most potent and popular brand I know of is Acetabolan, which is produced by MuscleTech. Not only does Acetabolan contain large doses of ALC, but it also includes several other essential synergistic nutrients that aid in ALC's effect. Acetabolan contains 100 percent pharmaceutical-grade ALC, branched-chain amino acids (valine, leucine, and isoleucine), zinc, taurine, ornithine alpha-ketoglutarate (OKG), and glutamine, which is the most abundant amino acid in the body. In fact, Acetabolan has the precise amount of glutamine (2,000 milligrams) that studies have shown elevates growth hormone levels.

This supplement should definitely be on every bodybuilder's check-it-out list. I confidently predict that ALC will soon be as popular among bodybuilders as creatine monohydrate has been during the past couple of years. If you've always wanted a natural and effective way of increasing your testosterone levels—and your muscle and strength gains—give ALC a try. Finally, there's a real alternative for natural bodybuilders.

Craig Titus.

Katy Rickman.

Chapter 10

PYRUVATE

BY CARLON COLKER, M.D., BETH ISRAEL MEDICAL CENTER, NEW YORK, AND PEAK WELLNESS, GREENWICH, CONNECTICUT

ROBERT STARK, M.D., F.A.C.C., PEAK WELLNESS, GREENWICH, CONNECTICUT, YALE UNIVERSITY SCHOOL OF MEDICINE

DOUGLAS KALMAN, M.S., R.D., PEAK WELLNESS, GREENWICH, CONNECTICUT

ALISA MINSCH, PEAK WELLNESS, GREENWICH, CONNECTICUT

ILENE WILETS, PH.D., BETH ISRAEL MEDICAL CENTER, NEW YORK

JAMES ROUFS, M.S., R.D., INTELLIGENT NUTRITION INC., BROOMFIELD, COLORADO

You've heard and probably read a lot about pyruvate lately, and rightly so. It's an amazing compound. After all, who isn't interested in something that's been touted as enhancing fat loss by 48 percent and increasing exercise endurance by 20 percent? According to the nine studies done with humans that have been published to date, however, the amount of pyruvate a person would have to ingest to achieve those results is just not practical. In fact, according to the studies, a person would have to ingest somewhere between 31 and 100 grams each day of either pyruvate or a mixture of pyruvate and dihydroxyacetone, a substance similar to pyruvate, in order to enhance weight loss and fat loss, increase exercise endurance and decrease fatigue levels.[1-9] There's no question the product works, but 31 to 100 grams is a lot to take every day—and it's costly. The real question is whether much smaller, more practical doses are also effective. One company set out to answer this question by putting its pyruvate formula through the rigors of a double-blind, placebo-controlled study, which was conducted at Peak Wellness, an independent, comprehensive research center in Greenwich, Connecticut.

SCIENCE PUTS PYRUVATE+™ TO THE TEST

The objective of this study was to evaluate the effects of a pyruvate-based formula—Pyruvate+, a product sold by New Vision International Inc., a network marketing company in Scottsdale, Arizona—on weight and body composition as well as on energy and fatigue levels in individuals who were 10 to 15 pounds overfat. The table in the right column shows that pyruvate is the primary component of the formula, which contains 1,200 milligrams of pyruvate per two capsules. It's also important to note that since two capsules provide 100 micrograms of chromium chelated to niacin and the amino acid glycine, as well as other ingredients, not all of the effects can be completely attributed to pyruvate. Consequently, the objective of the study was to evaluate the effectiveness of Pyruvate+, not just pyruvate. The results, however, would provide some evidence as to the effectiveness of doses much smaller than those used in the previous studies involving humans.

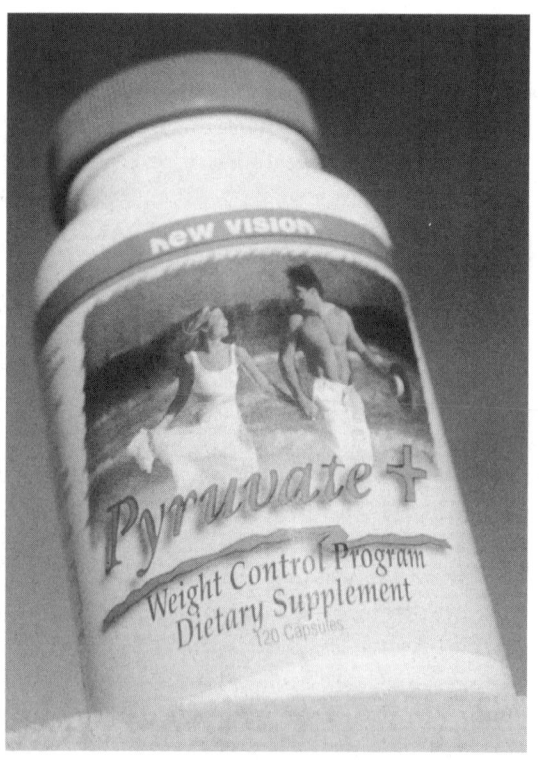

Pyruvate+ Formula	
Each two capsules contain	
Pyruvate (from calcium and sodium pyruvate)	1,200 milligrams
Calcium (from calcium pyruvate)	160 milligrams
Sodium (from sodium pyruvate)	30 milligrams
Zinc (from zinc oxide)	10 milligrams
Vitamin B$_6$ (as pyridoxine HCL)	3 milligrams
Chromium (from chromium dinicotinate/glycinate)	100 micrograms
Corn silk	60 milligrams
Uva ursi	20 milligrams
Cranberry powder	10 milligrams
Dihydroxyacetone (DHA)	10 milligrams

Study design

Fifty-three healthy individuals, with an average age of 36, were recruited for the study, including 25 females and 28 males. Each of the participants was approximately 10 to 15 pounds overfat, as determined by Body Mass Index (BMI). A commonly used method of estimating bodyfat level, BMI is determined by dividing a person's weight (in kilograms) by his or her height (in meters) squared to give a value of kg/m^2. In order to be part of the study, each subject had to have a BMI value of 25 or greater, which in the general population is associated with having 10 to 15 extra pounds of bodyfat.

Once the study was under way, the researchers got a more accurate measurement of bodyfat and lean body mass for each individual by bioelectric impedance analysis (BIA). The participants then met with a dietitian and an exercise physiologist who instructed them to follow a specific 2,000-calories-per-day diet as well as a defined five-days-a-week exercise program. The participants were then ran-

domly placed in one of three groups: a control group, a placebo group, or a Pyruvate+ group.

All three groups followed the same diet and exercise program for six weeks. The placebo group received 10 capsules a day of a placebo, or inactive substance, which was maltodextrin, a complex carbohydrate that provides approximately the same amount of calories as the Pyruvate+ product. The control group did not receive any of the capsules, and the Pyruvate+ group received 10 capsules of Pyruvate+ each day, which provides 6 grams of pyruvate. Neither the placebo group nor the Pyruvate+ group knew which capsules they were taking, since the study was double-blind (which means neither the participants in the

Jean-Pierre Fux.

Jean-Pierre Fux.

study nor the researchers themselves knew who was getting which capsules). This type of study design—double-blind, placebo-controlled—is considered the gold standard, since it removes both the participants' and the researchers' ability to bias the results.

While the specifics of how a study is set up are essential to understanding whether the results are trustworthy, they are certainly not as exciting as the results themselves, so let's take a look at what the study found.

EFFECTS OF PYRUVATE+ ON BODYWEIGHT AND BODY COMPOSITION

When all of the numbers were in and the statistics completed, no significant change in bodyweight was found in any of the three groups, including the Pyruvate+ group. Those results were somewhat surprising; however, despite the fact that there was no discernable change in bodyweight, there was a significant change in body composition. The researchers found that the participants ingesting Pyruvate+ lost 4.8 pounds of bodyfat during the six-week study, which translates into a weekly bodyfat loss of 0.8 pound. This loss of 4.8 pounds was quite a contrast with the gain of 0.1 pound in bodyfat found in the control group and the loss of 0.2 pound observed in the placebo group (see page 92). Furthermore, the 4.8-pound loss in bodyfat in six weeks becomes even more significant when you consider that the study participants were ingesting 2,000 calories a day and not the 500 or 1,000 calories used in some of the previous studies. The loss of 4.8 pounds of bodyfat resulting from ingesting Pyruvate+ for six weeks is, therefore, quite remarkable.

You may be thinking, "But I thought you said their weight didn't change." True, but the reason their weight didn't change despite a significant decrease in bodyfat is that the participants ingesting the Pyruvate+ also gained 3.4 pounds of lean body mass. This increase is in direct contrast to the small gain of 0.4 pound in the control group and the small loss of 0.3 pound in the placebo group

Jean-Pierre Fux.

(see page 92). Therefore, even though their weight didn't change significantly, the participants actually gained more than a half pound of lean body mass each week. It's also important to add that the study participants didn't engage in heavy-duty weight training. The increase in lean body mass occurred with just a 30-minute combination workout of aerobic and anaerobic exercise five days per week. Also note that all the participants went through the exact same workouts five days a week.

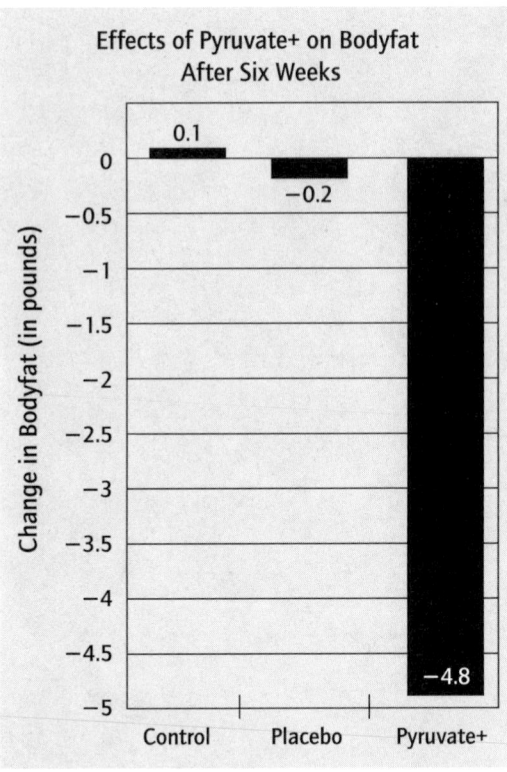

Effects of Pyruvate+ on Bodyfat After Six Weeks

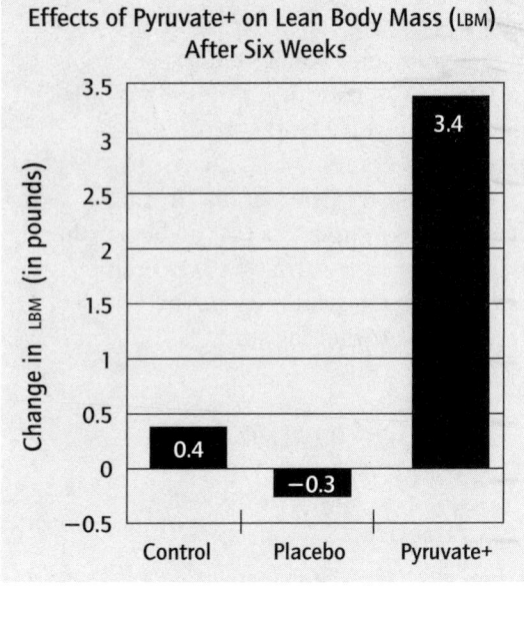

Effects of Pyruvate+ on Lean Body Mass (LBM) After Six Weeks

One method of summarizing changes in body composition, such as decreases in bodyfat and increases in lean body mass, involves a formula known as Body Composition Improvement, or BCI. The formula is rather simple in that for every pound of bodyfat people lose or gain, they are given a value: +1 if they lose a pound, and −1 if they gain a pound. Therefore, if a person loses 4.8 pounds of bodyfat, he or she is given a value of +4.8. This is then added to the amount of lean body mass a person gains or loses. If we add the 3.4 pounds of lean body mass gained over the six weeks by those taking Pyruvate+, the BCI score is 8.2 pounds—a 4.8-pound decrease in bodyfat added to a 3.4-pound increase in lean body mass. In contrast, the average BCI for the control group was +0.3 pound, and for the placebo group it was −0.1 pound. In more practical terms, a BCI score of +8.2 pounds simply means that the participants ingesting the Pyruvate+ were actually seeing a 1.4-pound positive change in their body composition each and every week of the six-week study while taking the product.

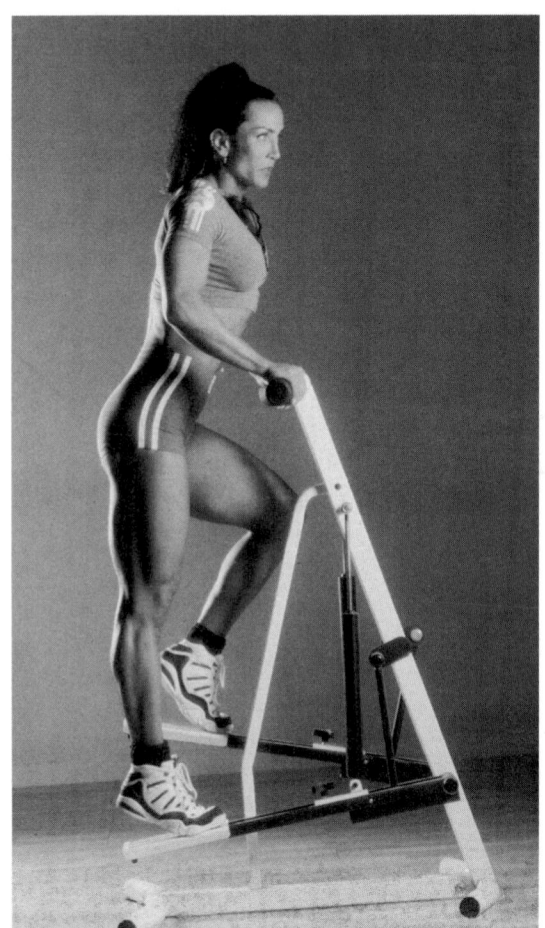

Laura Bass.

Chris Faildo.

Aaron Baker.

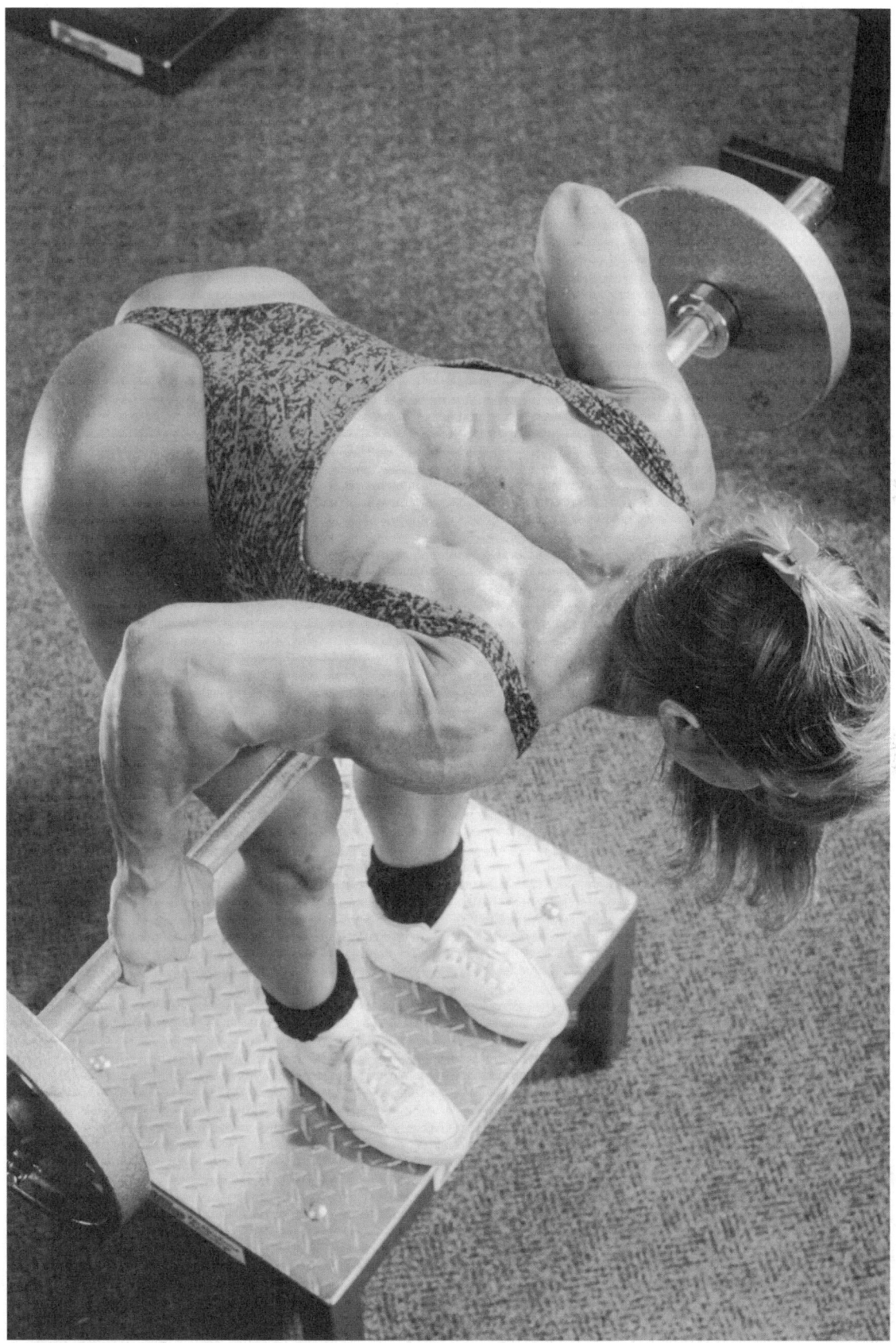

Rhonda Jorgenson.

The reason the BCI is such a good summary of what goes on when a person is trying to lose weight is that a person can lose a lot of weight, but much of that weight may or may not be bodyfat. In fact, the faster a person loses weight, the greater the tendency is that he or she will have to lose muscle in addition to losing some bodyfat. For example, let's say a person loses 10 pounds quite rapidly. At best 5 of those 10 pounds will be fat, while the other 5 will be water and muscle weight. Consequently, the BCI would be zero: $5 + (-5) = 0$. This is a situation no one should strive for, at least not if he or she wants to permanently solve the overfat condition.

Although most people are now beginning to realize that the enemy is bodyfat and not just weight, some still have a difficult time getting over what the scale says. The results of this study are perfect examples of how a person's body composition can change dramatically without his or her experiencing any significant change in bodyweight. The goal, therefore, should be to reduce bodyfat while maintaining or even increasing lean body mass.

It's no secret that we look and feel our best when we lose fat and maintain or even increase muscle mass, which is the primary reason most people lift weights and exercise—to look better. It's important to note, however, that since muscle is metabolically active and uses energy, losing muscle is actually counterproductive to losing bodyfat. On the other hand, maintaining or even increasing lean body mass has the opposite effect of maintaining and possibly even increasing metabolic rate, which simply makes it easier to achieve the look you strive for. The results of this double-blind, placebo-controlled study clearly demonstrate that Pyruvate+ not only enhances fat loss but also increases lean body mass at the same time.

Tatiana Anderson.

Melissa Coates.

Mia Finnegan.

EFFECTS OF PYRUVATE+ ON FATIGUE AND ENERGY LEVELS

The beneficial effects of reducing bodyfat and increasing lean body mass were not the only positive effects seen with Pyruvate+. The group ingesting the product also experienced an 18 percent increase in vigor, or energy levels. When compared with the increases of only 1.8 and 4.5 percent found in the control and placebo groups, respectively, this increased vigor was highly significant. The Pyruvate+ group also experienced a 71 percent decrease in fatigue levels. Intriguingly, the placebo group experienced a 48 percent reduction in

fatigue within six weeks, which simply illustrates the need for well-controlled studies like this one that use a placebo so that the results of the study are much more reliable and not simply due to a placebo effect.

These are the results of this study done with human subjects who were approximately 10 to 15 pounds overfat and ingested 10 capsules of Pyruvate+, which supplied 6 grams of pyruvate per day, for six weeks:

4.8-pound loss of bodyfat
3.4-pound increase in lean body mass
18 percent increase in energy levels
71 percent decrease in fatigue levels

Lee Labrada.

Although future research is required to determine whether these statistically significant benefits are due to the pyruvate, or the other ingredients in the product, such as chromium, or to the combination of them all, the study does clearly demonstrate the effectiveness of Pyruvate+. It's encouraging to see nutritional-supplement companies having the effectiveness of their products tested by independent research facilities.

References

1. Robertson, R. J., R. T. Stanko, F. L. Goss, R. J. Spina, J. J. Reilly, and K. D. Greenawalt. 1990. Blood glucose extraction as a mediator of perceived exertion during prolonged exercise. *European Journal of Applied Physiology.* 61:100–105.

2. Stanko, R. T., and J. E. Arch. 1996. Inhibition of regain in bodyweight and fat with addition of 3-carbon compounds to the diet with hyperenergetic refeeding after weight reduction. *International Journal of Obesity.* 20:925–930.

3. Stanko, R. T., A. Mitrakou, K. Greenawalt, and J. Gerich. 1990. Effect of dihydroxyacetone and pyruvate on plasma glucose concentration and turnover in noninsulin-dependent diabetes mellitus. *Clinical Physiology and Biochemistry.* 8:283–288.

4. Stanko, R. T., H. Reiss Reynolds, R. Hoyson, J. E. Janosky, and R. Wolf. 1994. Pyruvate supplementation of low-cholesterol, low-fat diet: Effects on plasma lipid concentrations and body composition in hyperlipidemic patients. *American Journal of Clinical Nutrition.* 59:423–427.

5. Stanko, R. T., H. Reiss Reynolds, K. D. Lonchar, and J. E. Arch. 1992. Plasma lipid concentrations in hyperlipidemic patients consuming a high-fat diet supplemented with pyruvate for six weeks. *American Journal of Clinical Nutrition.* 56:950–954.

6. Stanko, R.T., R. J. Robertson, R. W. Galbreath, J. J. Reilly, K. D. Greenawalt, and F. L. Goss. 1990. Enhanced leg exercise endurance with a high-carbohydrate diet and dihydroxyacetone and pyruvate. *Journal of Applied Physiology.* 69:1651–1656.

7. Stanko, R. T., R. J. Robertson, R. J. Spina, J. J. Reilly, K. D. Greenawalt, and F. L. Goss. 1990. Enhancement of arm exercise endurance capacity with dihydroxyacetone and pyruvate. *Journal of Applied Physiology.* 68:119–124.

8. Stanko, R. T., D. L. Teitze, and J. E. Arch. 1992a. Body composition, energy utilization, and nitrogen metabolism with a severely restricted diet supplemented with dihydroxyacetone and pyruvate. *American Journal of Clinical Nutrition.* 55:771–775.

9. Stanko, R. T., D. L. Teitze, and J. E. Arch. 1992b. Body composition, energy utilization, and nitrogen metabolism with a 4.25-MJ/d low-energy diet supplemented with pyruvate. *American Journal of Clinical Nutrition.* 56:630–635.

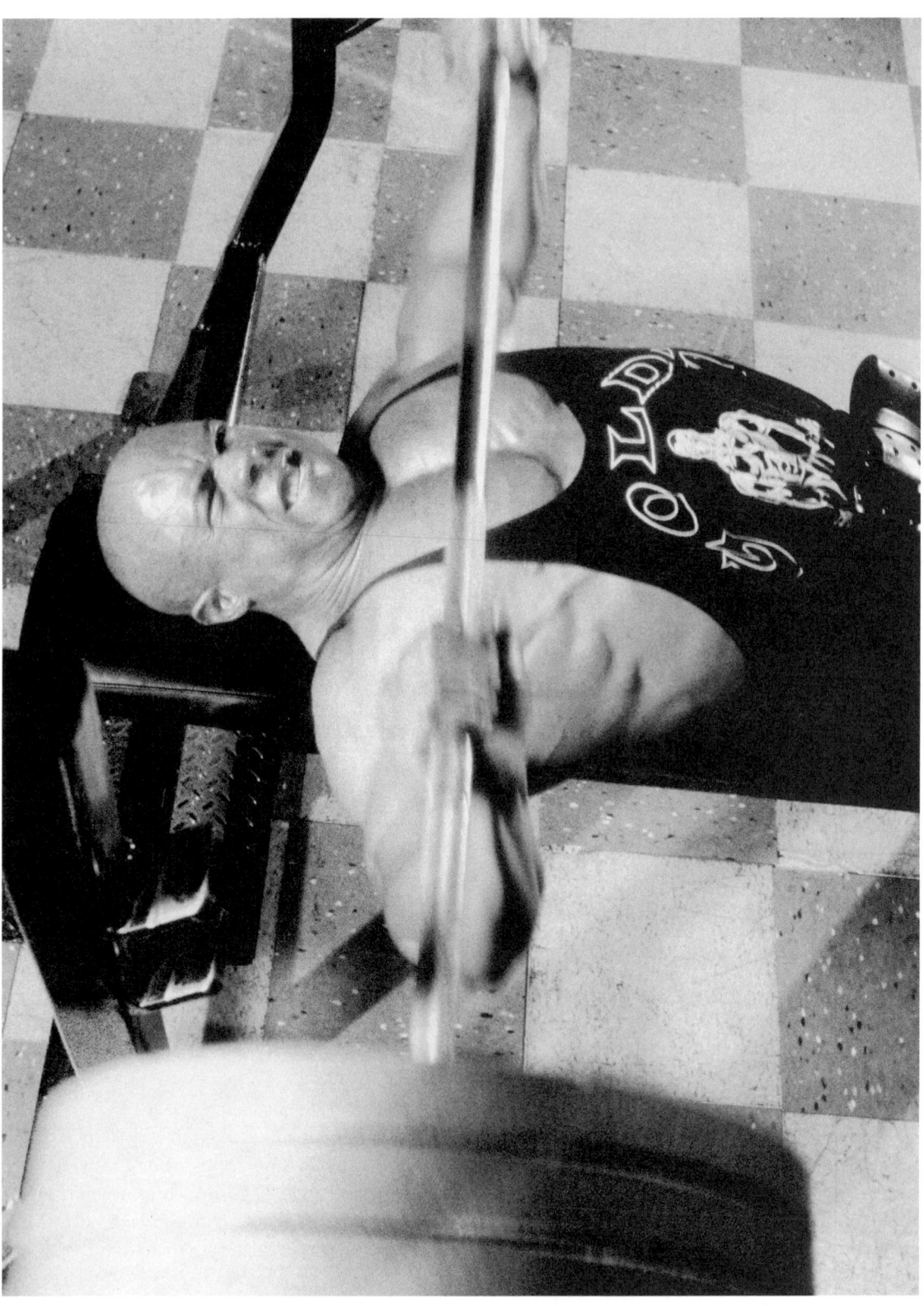

Skip La Cour.

Chapter 11

MASS MACHINE NUTRITION
DIET SECRETS TO HELP YOU GET BIG AND RIPPED

BY SKIP LA COUR

Eating is the most important part of a body-building program. In fact, some experts say that good nutrition accounts for up to 80 percent of the physique-developing process. Therefore, if you want quality muscle, you should direct most of your effort toward your eating habits.

There's no debate on that issue, in my opinion, although it does fly in the face of what many bodybuilders believe. Training is generally considered to be the most important aspect of our sport; however, weight training takes up only one to two hours a day, four to six days a week. What you do outside of those few short hours makes a big difference in your progress.

Based on my own experiences, I believe that poor or inconsistent nutritional habits are the reason many natural bodybuilders fail to achieve their full genetic potential. Many of us who train drug-free don't take complete responsibility for our lack of progress. We blame such factors as training plateaus, poor genetics, or the fact that we don't use drugs. The problem could well be, however, that we don't pay enough attention to the way we eat.

SCHEDULING MEALS

Feeding your body essential nutrients at regular intervals throughout the day is a key to building muscle. I suggest that you eat at least six times a day, or every two to three hours. For me, eating well equates to eight high-quality meals a day; that is, eating every two hours.

My meals are carefully balanced in terms of calories, protein, carbohydrates, and fat. The human body can use the nutrients more efficiently if they come in smaller, more frequent meals than in larger, less frequent ones. As someone once advised me, "Think of yourself as a steer, a horse, or some other grazing animal. They eat small amounts all day long, which help them build tremendously muscular and lean bodies." Since then, I have liked to refer to myself as a grazing steer whenever someone observes that I always seem to be eating.

You must keep your body fed with nutrient-dense foods, day in and day out. Seven days of quality meals create a quality week that is sure

Skip La Cour.

to contribute to your growth. Four weeks of that makes a great month, and 12 great months of eating well will create a great year of adding quality muscle. If you're committed enough to stack a few years together, you'll surely build a physique you can truly be proud of. That's the kind of consistency you need if you plan on achieving substantial growth without drugs. There are no shortcuts.

EATING WELL IS EASIER THAN YOU THINK

Eating to build muscle is a way of thinking just as much as it's an activity. Many bodybuilders are easily confused, frustrated, and even overwhelmed when it comes to proper nutrition. The process doesn't have to be so complicated. To create an effective nutritional program, you must determine three things:

1. The main purpose of each of the three macronutrients: protein, carbohydrates, and fat.

2. The number of calories you need to consume in order to meet your specific physique-enhancement goals.
3. The percentages of calories that should come from protein, carbohydrates, and fat.

Eating well seems much easier when you break it down that way, doesn't it? The question is, How do you calculate the total number of calories and determine the percentages of the macronutrients that will meet your body's needs?

The answers aren't necessarily easy to find, but with some experimentation, patience, and persistence, you'll figure out the best formula to help you reach your goals. Unfortunately, there's no way around the fact that you'll have to figure it out for yourself. There are no magic numbers that anyone can give you. The percentages not only vary from person to person, but they can also vary for the same person at different times. The guidelines in this chapter will give you an organized approach to determining what's best for you. You have to take it from there. This is where your fortitude and level of commitment come into play.

Be honest. Is the difficulty with this particular challenge one of understanding nutrition or one of following through with eating the way you know you should?

Eating is one of life's great pleasures. Sometimes, it's very difficult to stay away from great-tasting food that doesn't support your bodybuilding efforts. Even if you're committed to eating well, you sometimes find it difficult to break away from your busy schedule and eat a meal—whether it's good for you or not.

It comes down to motivation. This is a great time to determine exactly why you will absolutely *commit* to eating the way you should to build the physique you really want. If you know why you want to do something, it is that much easier to figure out how to do it.

MUSCLE IS PROTEIN

Protein is by far the number-one nutrient you need to build muscle. Muscle is protein. It's important to maintain a positive balance of nitrogen. You do that by taking in plenty of protein. Like many other bodybuilders, I've discovered that the more protein I consume, the bigger and stronger I get. You must experiment to determine the exact amount of protein you need to keep a positive protein balance for building muscle.

Start with one to 1.5 grams per pound of bodyweight—and move up from there. Many experts estimate that the average hard-training bodybuilder needs that much per day. If your body can efficiently use more, I suggest that you give it more.

There's another method of determining the proper amount of protein for bodybuilding; however, I don't believe such a cookie-cutter rule can possibly apply to everyone—especially every single hard-training bodybuilder. With this method you multiply your bodyweight in kilograms by 1.5 to determine your daily protein grams. (To figure your weight in kilograms, divide the number of pounds you weigh by 2.2.) If you do try that formula, be sure to experiment upward from there. You don't want to rob yourself of even an ounce of potential muscle.

I weigh about 240 pounds and I eat approximately 453 grams of protein a day. About 165 grams of that, or 36 percent, come from regular food like chicken, tuna, and egg whites. The other 288 grams, or 64 percent, come from high-quality whey protein in the form of convenient meal replacements and powders. I divide the protein as evenly as possible over the eight meals of my day.

The cost of protein is well worth the investment. I believe in maintaining a regular

---

Mass Machine Diets

Definition Diet (Regular Carbs Salad Day)

Meal and Time	Ingredients
Postworkout: 7 A.M.	2 servings whey protein in 1 quart water
Meal 1: 8 A.M.	Egg whites, broccoli, oatmeal, whey protein in 1 quart water
Meal 2: 10 A.M.	Meal replacement in 1 quart water
Meal 3: Noon	Chicken breast, salad (store-bagged lettuce, cucumber, balsamic vinegar), rice, whey protein in 1 quart water
Meal 4: 1 P.M.	Meal replacement in 1 quart water
Meal 5: 3 P.M.	Chicken breast, salad (store-bagged lettuce, cucumber, balsamic vinegar), rice, whey protein in 1 quart water
Meal 6: 5 P.M.	Meal replacement in 1 quart water
Meal 7: 7 P.M.	Chicken breast, salad (store-bagged lettuce, cucumber, balsamic vinegar), rice, whey protein in 1 quart water
Meal 8: 9 P.M.	Meal replacement in 1 quart water

Build Muscle, Lose Fat (Moderate Carbs Salad Day)

Meal and Time	Ingredients
Postworkout: 7 A.M.	2 servings whey protein in 1 quart water
Meal 1: 8 A.M.	Egg whites, broccoli, whey protein in 1 quart water
Meal 2: 10 A.M.	Meal replacement in 1 quart water
Meal 3: Noon	Chicken breast, salad (store-bagged lettuce, cucumber, balsamic vinegar), whey protein in 1 quart water
Meal 4: 1 P.M.	Meal replacement in 1 quart water
Meal 5: 3 P.M.	Chicken breast, salad (store-bagged lettuce, cucumber, balsamic vinegar), whey protein in 1 quart water
Meal 6: 5 P.M.	Meal replacement in 1 quart water
Meal 7: 7 P.M.	Chicken breast, salad (store-bagged lettuce, cucumber, balsamic vinegar), whey protein in 1 quart water
Meal 8: 9 P.M.	Meal replacement in 1 quart water

Mass Machine Diets (continued)

Quick-Cuts System (Low Calorie, Extremely Low Carbs)

Meal and Time	Ingredients
Postworkout: 7 A.M.	2 servings whey protein in 1 quart water
Meal 1: 8 A.M.	Egg whites, broccoli, whey protein in 1 quart water
Meal 2: 10 A.M.	Whey protein in 1 quart water
Meal 3: Noon	Chicken breast, salad (store-bagged lettuce, cucumber, balsamic vinegar), whey protein in 1 quart water
Meal 4: 1 P.M.	Whey protein in 1 quart water
Meal 5: 3 P.M.	Chicken breast, salad (store-bagged lettuce, cucumber, balsamic vinegar), whey protein in 1 quart water
Meal 6: 5 P.M.	Whey protein in 1 quart water
Meal 7: 7 P.M.	Chicken breast, salad (store-bagged lettuce, cucumber, balsamic vinegar), whey protein in 1 quart water
Meal 8: 9 P.M.	Whey protein in 1 quart water

Maintenance Program (Moderate Carbs)

Meal and Time	Ingredients
Postworkout: 7 A.M.	2 servings whey protein in 1 quart water
Meal 1: 8 A.M.	Egg whites, broccoli, 1 tablespoon canola oil, whey protein in 1 quart water
Meal 2: 10 A.M.	Meal replacement in 1 quart water
Meal 3: Noon	Chicken breast, salad (store-bagged lettuce, cucumber, balsamic vinegar), 1 tablespoon canola oil, whey protein in 1 quart water
Meal 4: 1 P.M.	Meal replacement in 1 quart water
Meal 5: 3 P.M.	Chicken breast, salad (store-bagged lettuce, cucumber, balsamic vinegar), 1 tablespoon canola oil, whey protein in 1 quart water
Meal 6: 5 P.M.	Meal replacement in 1 quart water
Meal 7: 7 P.M.	Chicken breast, salad (store-bagged lettuce, cucumber, balsamic vinegar), 1 tablespoon canola oil, whey protein in 1 quart water
Meal 8: 9 P.M.	Meal replacement in 1 quart water

Mass Machine Diets (continued)

Mass Builder (Higher Calories, Higher Carbs)

Meal and Time	Ingredients
Postworkout: 7 A.M.	2 servings whey protein in 1 quart water
Meal 1: 8 A.M.	Egg whites, broccoli, 1 tablespoon canola oil, rice, whey protein in 1 quart water
Meal 2: 10 A.M.	Meal replacement in 1 quart water
Meal 3: Noon	Chicken breast, salad (store-bagged lettuce, cucumber, balsamic vinegar), 1 tablespoon canola oil, rice, whey protein in 1 quart water
Meal 4: 1 P.M.	Meal replacement in 1 quart water
Meal 5: 3 P.M.	Chicken breast, salad (store-bagged lettuce, cucumber, balsamic vinegar), 1 tablespoon canola oil, rice, whey protein in 1 quart water
Meal 6: 5 P.M.	Meal replacement in 1 quart water
Meal 7: 7 P.M.	Chicken breast, salad (store-bagged lettuce, cucumber, balsamic vinegar), 1 tablespoon canola oil, rice, whey protein in 1 quart water
Meal 8: 9 P.M.	Meal replacement in 1 quart water

Cory Everson.

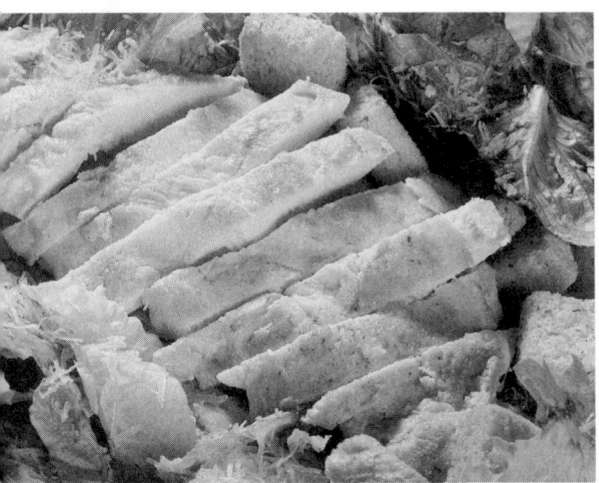

food budget, and supplementation spending should start with good high-quality protein. The higher the quality of the protein you put into your system, the more your body will use for growing muscle tissue and the less it will convert into fat. I'd go so far as to say that you should spend 75 percent of your food and supplement budget on protein.

CARBOHYDRATES

Carbohydrates give you the energy you need to carry out your everyday activities and train hard in the gym. Your body needs carbohydrates throughout the day to feed your brain, which uses glucose, or blood sugar, as its primary energy source. Glucose is a carbohydrate that every cell in your body uses as fuel.

When your carbohydrate stores are depleted too far, your body converts precious muscle-building protein into glucose for the energy it needs. Obviously, that's something you want to avoid. Therefore, you have to eat enough carbohydrates to prevent it from happening.

Excess carbohydrates, however, get converted into fat. How can you avoid eating too many carbohydrates? One trick I've learned is to eat most of my carbohydrates in the morning and immediately after my workout—when my body processes them much more rapidly.

Some people advise limiting your carbohydrate consumption after 6 or 7 P.M. because they believe that carbs are converted to bodyfat much more easily at that time of day. Eating carbs at night reduces your body's ability to burn fat while you sleep. Others, however, have a different opinion. They say it doesn't really matter when you eat carbohydrates. Your body processes the carbohydrates the same way at any time.

How much carbohydrate should you eat? Here's the way I figure my own carb intake. As a bodybuilder I always keep my protein intake high. If getting or staying lean is a priority, I monitor the amount of fat in my diet. That leaves carbohydrates. I eat enough carbohydrates to give me energy to support my training intensity, meet the needs of all my other activities, and manage my bodyfat level—and not much more than that.

Lee Labrada.

FATS

Dietary fat has a vital purpose. It's a structural component of cell membranes and it supplies necessary chemical substrates for hormone production. Furthermore, fat protects vital organs and carries fat-soluble vitamins.

In other words, your body needs fat! Don't try to avoid it completely. Many experts feel that 26 to 30 percent of your total calories should come from fat.

There are two types of fat: saturated fat, which is considered bad, and unsaturated fat, which is considered good. Some people add olive oil and canola oil directly to their diets. I sometimes add the supplement conjugated linoleic acid (CLA) because I realize that fats are important to my overall health. CLA is generally accepted as being the good component of fat that regulates the metabolism of fat and protein. It may promote your gaining lean muscle and help your losing bodyfat. Studies have also shown CLA to have anticatabolic, antioxidant, and anticancer effects.

DETERMINING YOUR PERCENTAGES OF NUTRIENTS

The experts in the health and fitness community often debate what percentages of protein, carbs, and fats people should eat. The amounts you need are probably based on your body's ability to metabolize nutrients and on your particular fitness goals. Determining these amounts calls for experimentation.

At this point I hope I've hammered home my belief that you need to eat more protein than the average person does. Carbohydrates come second to ensure you have enough energy to support all your activities. When it comes to fat, however, you want to vary the amounts you take in, depending on the degree of leanness you want.

Take a look at the diets in this chapter, and you'll see that sometimes I add fat and sometimes I cut it out as much as possible, relying only on the fat in chicken breasts and other protein sources. I don't believe that you have to maintain an exact ratio of macronu-

Dave Palumbo.

trients to gain quality muscle mass. My numbers, however, usually total about 55 percent protein, 30 percent carbohydrates, and 15 percent fat.

How many calories do you need to build muscle?

For eating to gain muscle, the best—and the simplest—advice I've ever received came from Paul Delia, the president of AST Sports Science and the man most responsible for my development as a drug-free bodybuilder. "Skip," he said, "don't eat to get fat. Don't eat to stay lean. Eat to grow!"

Many bodybuilders are confused when it comes to eating the right amount of food to build quality muscle. One thing is certain: the

Mike Matarazzo.

scale is not a good indicator that you're adding muscle. It can't tell you how your training and nutritional habits are affecting your body composition; that is, the ratio of muscle to bodyfat. You may mistakenly think a rise in weight means you've put on some muscle when it's actually mostly bodyfat. On the other hand, many bodybuilders who have obviously gained lots of muscle and lost a considerable amount of bodyfat become discouraged because they aren't gaining weight. The best way to monitor your progress is to use the mirror. If you are a quantitative kind of guy or gal who can only relate to numbers, you may want to have an underwater-immersion fat analysis done to measure your progress accurately.

You often hear about bodybuilders who eat up to 10,000 calories a day. That's a *lot* of food! At my bodyweight, my calories normally range from 3,000 to 5,000 a day.

Can you build muscle and lose bodyfat at the same time?

The answer is yes—and it may be a lot less complicated than you might think.

To initiate the muscle-building process, you must constantly overload your muscles. Heavy, intense training is of utmost importance—so hit the weights hard in the gym.

To lose bodyfat and still gain muscle, you must keep your intake of quality protein high and, of course, watch your fat intake. Be aware, however, that the key to losing bodyfat may lie in your carbohydrate consumption—not only the amount of carbohydrates you eat but also the type. Your body cannot burn fat when your insulin levels are elevated—and carbohydrates raise your insulin levels. Consequently, you have to trick your body by varying the amount of carbs you take in.

Here's one strategy I suggest for manipulating your carbohydrate consumption: Eat only vegetables for carbohydrates for a couple of days. Then go back to a moderate amount of carbs like rice, Cream of Rice, Cream of Wheat, potatoes, and pasta for a couple of days. Alternate in that manner and see how quickly you start melting the fat. Because your

body needs carbohydrates for energy, the alternation may become difficult at times. Nevertheless, this method is effective.

The experts offer many different strategies for fat loss.

- Restricting dietary fat is a very common technique. It's obviously the first place to start cutting when you plan your eating regimen. Don't necessarily count on low fat alone, however. Many studies have shown that fat does not necessarily make you fat.[1]
- Eating carbs at certain times is another strategy. For example, restricting the amount of carbohydrates you eat later in the day is thought to put your body in a more advantageous position to

Jean-Pierre Fux.

Arne List.

Craig Titus.

burn calories more efficiently and prevent them from being stored as fat.[2]

- Some say it's all a matter of reducing the calories you eat and burning off more than you eat. The goal is to restrict your total calories for the day, and it doesn't matter whether those calories come from protein, carbohydrates, or fat.

My advice for gaining muscle and losing fat is simple: Keep your training as intense and heavy as possible. Slowly start reducing your calories by about 200 a day every week, cutting evenly from protein, carbohydrates, and fats—but make sure you're still getting high-quality protein. Then start experimenting with the amounts and types of carbohydrates you eat.

SKIP LA COUR'S TOP 10 BODYBUILDING NUTRITION TIPS

1. Make a list of all the reasons why now is the time to commit to eating right in order to build an outstanding physique. When you have a strong enough why, it's much easier to figure out how. Motivation—not a special diet secret—is the key to success here.

2. Keep your menus simple. The less planning and work you have to do when it comes to feeding yourself properly, the better. Try to look at eating as merely a method of building quality muscle, fueling great workouts, and keeping your body lean and looking good—instead of as a source of recreation, pleasure, and a means of connecting with your family and friends. I realize that delicious dining is one of life's great pleasures, but try thinking of yourself as an efficient muscle-building eater as much as possible.

3. Be consistent with your good eating habits. How well you eat during a particular day or even a week is easily neutralized by just a few bad days. Make a good day of eating stretch into a good week, a good week into a good

Monica Brant.

month, and several good months into a good year. That's when you'll start seeing the improvements you desire.

4. Build your nutritional program around a solid foundation of high-quality protein. Muscle is made of protein, so protein builds muscle.

5. When you're trying to lose bodyfat, concentrate primarily on reducing overall calories. Many people place too much importance on reducing fats and carbohydrates. Start the fat-loss

Sue Price.

process by simply reducing your calories.

6. Pay special attention to the way your body processes carbohydrates. Barry Sears, author of *Enter the Zone*, believes that 25 percent of people process carbohydrates efficiently while the rest of us don't process them very well.[2] Experiment with different types and amounts of carbohydrates to see what works best for your body.

7. Weight gain does not necessarily mean muscle gain. Be sure to train as heavily as possible, eat high-quality protein, and add enough carbohydrates to give yourself energy to live the life and look the way you want. And, of course, watch your fat intake. Forget about the scale! Use the mirror as your guide.

8. Advanced planning is essential. That's especially true when you have an extremely busy schedule or when you're traveling. Know in advance what you'll eat on a particular day. Don't wait to figure out what you're going to do about eating.

9. Take advantage of meal replacements, high-quality whey protein, and even the convenient protein bars. With the tremendous accessibility of such products, there's little reason to miss out on your daily requirements of the most important bodybuilding nutrient.

10. Plan your cheat days in advance too. Set up your nutritional plan to be a series of sprints, rather than an endless marathon. By doing so, you'll be more likely to adhere to your plan. You'll know in advance that you can soon reward yourself for exhibiting incredible discipline. There's nothing like a Saturday for eating like a pig, if you want, after being a disciplined eating Mass Machine all week long!

References

1. Carmichael, H. E., et al. 1998. Lower fat intake as a predictor of initial and sustained weight loss in obese subjects consuming an otherwise ad libitum diet. *Journal of American Dieticians Association*. 35–39.

2. Sears, B. 1995. *Enter the Zone*. New York: HarperCollins Publishers.

Rich Piana.

Chapter 12

THE GROWTH HORMONE PHENOMENON

BY STEVE HOLMAN

Hormone manipulation may sound like some futuristic concept, but it's here—and it's achieving spectacular results in medicine and athletics. In terms of muscle development, the technique of boosting testosterone, growth hormone, and insulin levels at specific times is becoming the great bodybuilding equalizer. Thanks in part to hormone manipulation, we're now seeing some of the most impressive drug-free bodybuilders that ever walked planet Earth. Studies show over and over again that boosting certain hormones can produce results similar to those that occur with anabolic steroid use.

Is hormone manipulation as dangerous as steroid use? Not in most cases. In fact, if you train intensely with weights, you already manipulate your hormones to a degree. Intense weight training increases both testosterone and growth hormone output, which is one reason you get results. If you're like most mass-hungry bodybuilders, however, you're looking to kick up those results a few notches—and perhaps uncover the key to ultimate size and strength.

Your growth hormone level is critical to your getting spectacular results with hormone manipulation. It's the orchestra leader that conducts the other hormones, the quarterback leading the anabolic drive.

For example, a high GH level helps amplify the anabolic response of testosterone. It can also deter many of the anticatabolic (or "anti-muscle-wasting") effects of cortisol: when GH is high, cortisol is low. The anabolic/anticatabolic power of GH makes it the premier bodybuilding hormone, and you should attempt to boost it as often as possible.

How do you up your GH and increase the power of your other anabolic hormones without having to resort to injections? Proper training is the place to start.

BOOST YOUR GH IN THE GYM

Three training variables have a direct impact on growth hormone and its positive effects on muscle hypertrophy: intensity, muscle stretch, and muscle burn. When you combine them

Don Long.

during your workouts, you create an extreme anabolic environment.

Intensity As James Jamieson (noted pharmacologist and developer of GH Stak, the growth hormone supplement) and Dr. Lawrence Dorman (a leader in the field of natural medicine) write in their book *Growth Hormone: The Methuselah Factor*, "Sustained high-intensity exercise increases the quantity and number of pulses of GH release. Intense is the key word here; garden-variety jogging won't do it." That means you need focused effort on the big compound weight-training movements to affect your GH levels.

Yes, you've read it many times in *Ironman*, but it can't be overstated. Intense effort on the big exercises is vital—for example, squats for your quads, bench presses for your chest, overhead presses for your delts, and rows and chins for your back. If you want an increase in GH, use the core movements in the majority of your bodypart programs.

Jean-Pierre Fux.

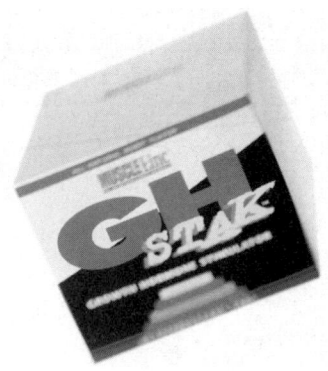

Muscle Stretch Stretch-position movements, such as stiff-legged deadlifts for the hamstrings and flyes for the pecs, can increase the IGF-1 receptors on the muscles. IGF-1, or insulin-like growth factor 1, is a highly anabolic metabolite that can occur as a direct result of higher GH output, and it can have a tremendous positive impact on muscle growth. Here's a list of stretch-position movements for each bodypart. Seriously consider incorporating them all into your program for maximum growth response from your higher GH level.

Jean-Pierre Fux and Karin Scheuber.

Quads:	Sissy squats
Hamstrings:	Stiff-legged deadlifts
Calves:	Donkey calf raises, leg-press calf raises
Chest:	Flyes
Lats:	Pullovers
Midback:	Close-grip cable rows
Delts:	One-arm incline laterals
Biceps:	Incline dumbbell curls
Triceps:	Overhead extensions
Abs:	Full-range crunches, Ab-bench crunch pulls

One highly effective way to use these exercises is to do a few sets of the corresponding stretch-position exercise at the end of each bodypart routine. For example, end your chest workout with two sets of flyes, and on your last set emphasize a stretch-pause on each rep, holding for a four-count in the stretch position before continuing the movement. Stretch-pauses can increase the IGF-1 receptor development and stimulate an even greater anabolic response.

Katy Rickman.

Muscle Burn In a study published in the *Canadian Journal of Applied Physiology* (1997, 22:244–255), researchers showed a direct correlation between higher lactic acid levels in the blood and GH release from the pituitary gland. That means the more muscle burn you induce, the more growth hormone you can stimulate. To attain the searing effect efficiently, "superset" two exercises in each bodypart routine. For example, use a multijoint exercise (such as bench presses) and follow it immediately with a lighter, single-joint or contracted-position movement (such as cable crossovers). That superset, a variation of the "Aftershock" technique, will trigger the higher lactic acid levels you're after.

Put these three variables together, and your GH-boosting quad routine might look like the following:

Exercise	Sets and Reps
Squats (warm-up)	2 × 15
Aftershock superset	2 × 6–9
Leg presses	1–2 × 7
Leg extensions	1–2 × 7
Sissy squats	1 × 12
Sissy squats (stretch-pause)	1 × 6

Here's a sample arm routine:

Exercise	Sets and Reps
Triceps	
Decline extensions	2 × 6–9
Aftershock superset	
Close-grip bench presses	1 × 7
Dumbbell kickbacks	1 × 7
Overhead extensions	1 × 9
Overhead extensions (stretch-pause)	1 × 6
Biceps	
Barbell curls	2 × 6–9
Aftershock superset	
Undergrip pulldowns	1 × 7
Spider curls*	1 × 7
Incline curls	1 × 9
Incline curls (stretch-pause)	1 × 6

*Performed on the vertical side of a preacher bench.

SUPPLEMENTS TO RAMP UP GH: NO INJECTIONS NECESSARY

There have been a number of studies showing that specific amino acids, such as glutamine, can boost GH output. One supplement that incorporates the known GH releasers in a powerful compound is GH Stak, a.k.a. Pro-HGH Symbiotropin.

Bodybuilders at the *Ironman* Training & Research Center have been experimenting with this compound—effervescent tablets, like Alka-Seltzer, that you dissolve in water and drink on an empty stomach either before you train or at bedtime. Drug-free bodybuilder Jonathan Lawson made some spectacular gains using GH Stak, adding more than 10 pounds of muscle to his ripped competition

Chris Faildo.

Jean-Pierre Fux.

weight. He competed in 1997 at a bodyweight
of just over 180 pounds, and with his first
eight-week cycle of GH Stak he boosted that to
a ripped-and-ready 195 pounds in early 1998.
He got that amazing result due to a number of
factors, including the supplement and his
high-intensity, full-range training protocol,
which incorporated the concepts you just read
about. Jamieson has said on many occasions
that you get a synergistic effect from the combination of the compounds in the effervescent
supplement and the GH-releasing effects of
high-intensity exercise. Lawson certainly did.

Why does GH Stak come in an effervescent form? Studies have shown that there's a
significant increase in GH from oral glutamine
when the glutamine is in that form—due
to pH manipulation in the stomach—and
significantly better absorption. The effervescent action also enhances the delivery of

Johnny Stewart, 1998 Middleweight Team Universe
Champion.

Chris Faildo.

other growth hormone precursors in GH Stak, such as L-arginine, which is included in a more bioactive pyroglutamate form than you get from standard L-arginine supplements. Other GH Stak ingredients include glycine; tyrosine; aminotrope 7, a sequenced gly-coamino acid–complex; and compounds from a legume called the lacuna bean, which is naturally high in L-dopa, a renowned GH-stimulating compound.

GH Stak also contains anterior pituitary peptides that normalize somatostatin, a hor-mone that can shut down GH and IGF-1 receptors. That's critically important because when you elevate GH and IGF-1, you don't want somatostatin to smother their effects. GH Stak's anterior pituitary peptides prevent

the shutdown, which drastically increases the effects.

As for the research, Jamieson and Dorman presented a study to the American College for Advancement in Medicine, "The Role of Somatotroph-Specific Peptides and IGF-1 Intermediates as an Alternative to HGH Injections." In the 1997 study, a group of sub-jects took the supplement for 12 weeks, and while many of them were older individuals, there were young bodybuilders as well. Even though bodybuilders usually have higher-than-normal IGF-1 levels, the ones in the study still showed anywhere from a 12 percent increase in IGF-1 levels after just one day of using the supplement all the way to a 36.6 per-cent increase after only six days. Those are incredible numbers, especially when you realize there was no IGF-1 deficit to begin with. Most of the subjects who had low IGF-1 levels got even better results, with one showing almost a 230 percent increase in only 22 days (see table below).

Results with GH Stak have been so spectacular that doctors at antiaging clinics are using it in place of GH injections. That indicates that the medical community is embracing this supplement as a true alternative. In other words, it works.

Here's the bottom line for bodybuilders. Most pros inject GH, and many experts believe it's the very reason we see such incredibly massive competitors in the sport. It's believed that in combination with testosterone and other anabolic, anticatabolic compounds, the muscle-building power of GH is significantly increased (as are its fat-burning effects). GH also amplifies the power of many supplements—even protein powders. It's not hard to see why so many drug-using bodybuilders spend so much money on synthetic GH. If natural bodybuilders are going to come close to mimicking the powerful anabolic effect the pros get with synthetic GH injections and

steroids, they'll do it by combining growth hormone boosters, such as GH Stak, with testosterone boosters, scientifically designed protein powders, and cortisol suppressors. Hormone manipulation is the key to rapid drug-free muscle growth, and it's here in full force. It appears to be the anabolic trigger that natural bodybuilders have been frantically seeking.

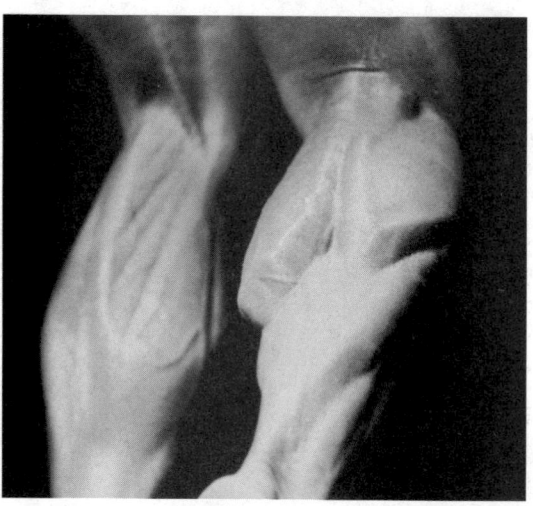

Physician-Supervised Clinical Studies: Pro-HGH™, a.k.a. GH Stak™				
Patients	Pre IGF-1 Test	Post IGF-1 Test	% Change	# of Days
Patient 1	73 on 1/14/97	141 on 1/25/97	+93.2%	11 days
Patient 2	21 on 1/14/97	69 on 2/05/97	+228.5%	22 days
Patient 3	110 on 1/18/97	180 on 2/04/97	+63.6%	18 days
Patient 4	357 on 1/24/97	388 on 1/25/97	+8.7%	1 day
Patient 5	167 on 1/24/97	178 on 1/25/97	+6.6%	1 day
Patient 6	242 on 1/24/97	273 on 1/25/97	+12.8%	1 day
Patient 7	255 on 1/24/97	269 on 1/29/97	+5.5%	2 days
Patient 8	93 on 1/31/97	127 on 2/05/97	+36.6%	6 days
Overall average IGF-1 increase: +56.9 percent		Overall average days: 7.75		

Note: Patients 1, 2, 3, 4, and 6 originally had low levels of IGF-1. Patients 5, 7, and 8 were healthy bodybuilders who were tested to monitor the immediate effects of Pro-HGH, a.k.a. GH Stak, on physically fit patients.

Chapter 13

MUSCLE WITHOUT MEAT

BY DANIEL CURTIS

When you look at someone as huge as Dorian Yates, you have to wonder how much meat he eats in a day. Most bodybuilders do eat a considerable amount of meat, poultry, and fish to build and maintain their massive physiques, but is eating animal flesh essential to building muscle? Protein is essential; animal flesh is not.

The trick is in getting enough high-quality protein from nonanimal sources. Even vegetarians who have never touched a barbell find it difficult to meet the recommended dietary allowance for protein, let alone consume the amount required for building huge muscles—but it can be done. It just takes careful planning.

Most bodybuilders know that they must take in all eight essential amino acids in order to increase their muscle tissue. While the experts used to say that you had to ingest all the essential aminos at one time, recent evidence suggests that isn't necessarily so. You can eat fruit, cereal, and toast for breakfast, a rela-

tively low-protein meal, as long as you eat the missing amino acids at lunch—say, in the form of nuts or legumes—so that protein will be formed and used for protein functions, including building muscle. That can be an advantage for the average vegan trying to consume 60 grams of protein per day, but it doesn't much help the bodybuilding vegan who needs double or triple that amount.

Vegans are total vegetarians, and they avoid eggs and dairy products as well as meat, poultry, and fish. To maximize total daily protein intake, vegan bodybuilders should consume all eight essential amino acids at every meal. Fortunately, science and food technology have worked together recently to make high-protein vegetarian foods more appealing to the American public. Although the primary targets for these foods are people who are at risk for heart disease and cancer—especially prostate and breast cancer—a pleasant side effect is the availability of high-protein vegetarian foods that taste good.

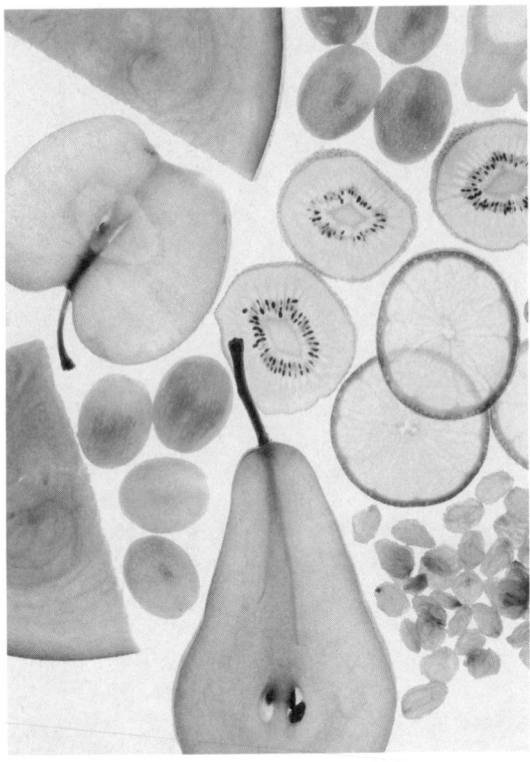

Debi Lee.

VARIETY OF PROTEINS

While soy milk and tofu have long been available in health-food stores, such new entrees as tofu lasagna, ravioli, and stroganoff (and a variety of vegeburgers, milkshakelike drinks, and yogurtlike desserts) are now available even in supermarkets. There are also more cookbooks that feature soy protein recipes. So far, the public's response has been very good.

Legumes

Legumes are another protein staple for the vegan. The endless varieties available include pinto beans, garbanzo beans, kidney beans, great white northern beans, and black beans, as well as lentils and split peas. You can use them in soups, in burritos, or baked in sauces. You can also boil and mash them and make refried beans, serving them with rice, as in traditional Mexican cooking. The quality of legume protein increases measurably if you eat it with a grain-based food, such as rice, bread, or tortillas. If you're new to legumes, to avoid intestinal discomfort start with a small amount, such as a quarter cup, and work up gradually or take Beano, a product that reduces gas. You'll be more comfortable, as will the people around you.

James Demelo.

Nuts, seeds, and butters

Nuts, seeds, and nut butters are protein powerhouses for vegans as well. While the general public tends to limit nut consumption, due to the high fat content, the fat works for, rather than against, vegan bodybuilders. Even if you can triple your protein intake with vegetarian protein foods, you won't benefit fully if your calorie intake falls short. Your body will be forced to use your protein calories for energy, rather than muscle building, to make up for the shortage. The oils found in nuts and seeds are primarily monounsaturated, like olive oil, so they're heart friendly. They provide some fiber as well, and their protein and fat contents make them a must for bodybuilding vegans.

Powders

There are also a number of vegetarian protein powders on the market that are made of soy protein isolate—another must. Such products are an easy way to get top-quality protein into your diet. You just add water, juice, or soy milk.

If you train intensely for more than an hour a day, however, it will take more than vegetarian protein powder to build muscle. As mentioned above, you'll need a tremendous number of calories to fuel your workouts. An intake of 150 grams of protein, which would normally be adequate for muscle building, won't do you much good if you're eating only 2,000 to 2,500 calories a day. Depending on the intensity and duration of your workouts, your calorie range should be closer to 3,000 to 4,000 per day.

VEGETARIAN MUSCLE-BUILDING DIET

Getting adequate calories takes some creative planning, as most vegetarian foods, though healthy, tend to be low in calories. Don't skimp on such items as nuts, nut butters, olive oil, canola oil, and avocados. The following sample diet should give you some ideas.

Breakfast

Fresh fruit
3 slices (or more) 100 percent whole wheat toast
3 tablespoons natural, old-fashioned peanut butter
3 teaspoons canola oil margarine

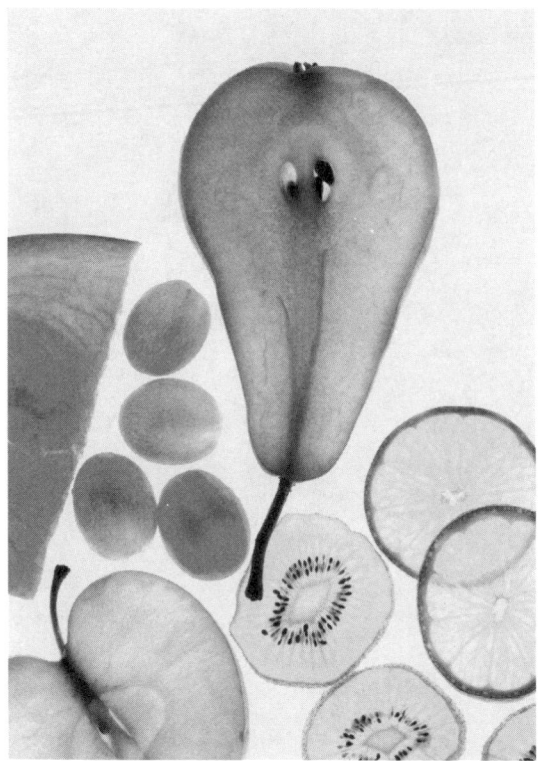

Dinner

Vegetarian entree, such as tofu lasagna
2 or 3 slices 100 percent whole-grain bread or
　whole-grain rolls
Canola oil margarine
Vegetable of choice
Salad with avocado slices
Olive oil–based dressing
Fresh fruit
8 ounces soy milk, Vitamite, or rice milk
　mixed with 1 tablespoon soy protein isolate
　(vegetarian protein powder)
1 banana

2 cups whole-grain cereal*
Milk**, soy milk, Vitamite milk substitute, or
　rice milk for cereal
8 ounces soy milk, Vitamite milk substitute, or
　rice milk mixed with
1 tablespoon soy protein isolate (vegetarian
　protein powder)
1 banana

*Examples include Wheaties, Grape Nuts, Mueslix, Wheat
Chex, bran flakes, and low-fat granola.

**If you eat dairy products.

Lunch

1 vegeburger, 2 vegetarian hot dogs, or 1 tofu
　cheese sandwich
Vegetarian chili
Green salad with avocado slices
Olive oil– or canola oil–based dressing
Fresh fruit
Tofu ice cream or yogurtlike dessert
Protein drink***

***Sorbet, juice, and 1 to 2 tablespoons soy protein
　isolate.

Craig Titus.

Danny Hester.

Snacks (1 to 3 per day)

Snack 1—Trail Mix

$^1/_4$ cup dry-roasted, unsalted peanuts
$^1/_4$ cup dry-roasted, unsalted cashews
$^1/_4$ cup dry-roasted, unsalted sunflower
    seeds
$^1/_4$ cup raisins

Snack 2—Peanut Butter and Crackers

2–3 tablespoons natural, old-fashioned
    peanut or almond butter
12 (or more) low-sodium wheat crackers
Soy milk or rice milk

Amy Lynn.

Danny Hester.

Snack 3—Apples and Mix

Apple slices, dipped in a mixture of:
    2 tablespoons nut butter
    1 tablespoon honey
    1 tablespoon sunflower seeds
    $^1/_4$ banana, mashed
    Vitamite mixed with sorbet
    1 tablespoon soy protein isolate

Will Willis.

Chapter 14

DYNAMIC CORTISOL CONTROL

BY MICHAEL GÜNDILL

Cortisol is considered the enemy of lean muscle mass. The popular theory states that the less cortisol your body produces, the better. In fact, chemically assisted bodybuilders lead the way in the battle against cortisol, and many don't hesitate to use dangerous drugs in an attempt to inhibit their natural secretion of the stress hormone. Drug-free bodybuilders also seek ways to suppress their cortisol secretion. The trouble is, the effects of cortisol on the human body aren't all bad. Some of its actions are positive and tend to help build muscle. So instead of looking for ways to block cortisol secretion, you should strive for dynamic cortisol control.

CORTISOL AND FAT

Fat specialists tell you that cortisol is a lipolytic hormone, which means it favors fat loss. That's true especially in a test tube—although specialists also point out that people who are obliged to use synthetic cortisol to treat various illnesses build up fat at a tremendous rate,

even if their diets don't change. It's almost impossible to get rid of the fat gained due to synthetic glucocorticoids, so, if there's a rationale for suppressing cortisol, it's the hormone's effect on adiposity.

The amazing thing is that suppressing cortisol production won't make you any leaner. That's the first paradox of cortisol. An excess of cortisol will make you fat; a lack of it, if anything, will also make you fat.

Cortisol and catabolism

Most bodybuilders associate cortisol with catabolism, and it's true that studies have shown that animals or sedentary people given cortisol see their muscle mass shrink. Muscle cells contain receptors that bind to cortisol. When that happens, it activates a very strong proteolytic pathway called the ATP-dependent ubiquitin/proteasome pathway, which causes the body to literally eat its own muscles.

The good news is that weight training impairs some of the direct catabolic actions of

Darrem Charles.

Debby McKnight.

cortisol. By putting regular tension on your muscles, you prevent the muscle cortisol receptors from working properly. It isn't a complete inhibition, though, because training tends to stimulate cortisol release. That's the second paradox of cortisol: Training both reduces cortisol's direct catabolic impact on muscle and increases the body's secretion of it. The more you train, the less cortisol-based muscle loss you'll experience. Unfortunately, more training also means more cortisol secretion, and the extra cortisol overrides the natural defense exerted by training.

Cortisol and anabolism

Another nasty effect of cortisol is that it slows the anabolic drive. Part of that antianabolic action is mediated directly through the muscle cortisol receptors, and training prevents that action. The problem is that another part of

Craig Titus.

WHAT ABOUT SUPPRESSING CORTISOL?

If cortisol can promote protein degradation and at the same time impair protein synthesis, you'd be wise to get rid of it, wouldn't you? There's some scientific basis to that reasoning. Animal-based studies reveal that suppressing the release of cortisol or inhibiting its actions by blocking cortisol receptors leads to increased muscle mass. For example, an amazing Canadian study involved four groups of 10 rats.[1] One was a control group, another was made up of severely burned rats, a third included rats that were burned but also received RU486 (the abortion pill that blocks cortisol receptors), and the fourth comprised rats that were uninjured and were given the RU486. Which group of rats had the most muscle at the end of the experiment? The rats that were severely burned but received RU486. They had even more muscle than the uninjured RU486 rats. That means RU486 not only eliminates the muscle loss due to stress (in this case a severe burn, although it could have been training), but it also promotes muscle gains. The problem with this study is that rats don't respond to cortisol in the same way that humans do, so the results won't necessarily apply to people.

Bodybuilders have used this synthetic cortisol receptor blocker without much success, and RU486's failure was attributed to its properties that stimulate cortisol release. When cortisol receptors are blocked, the body rapidly

cortisol's antianabolic action is indirect. Cortisol inhibits the release of numerous anabolic hormones, including growth hormone, insulin-like growth factor 1, and testosterone. It has also been shown to fight the androgen-receptor upregulation induced by nontraumatic workouts.

While training can partially inhibit some of the direct antianabolic effects of cortisol by impairing cortisol receptor responses, such preventive effects are localized in the trained muscles only. Training cannot overcome the unwelcome indirect effects of cortisol on the various anabolic hormones.

Jodi Friedman.

Cortisol and protein absorption

Scientists have known for a long time that eating a meal triggers the release of cortisol. They've also discovered that proteins are the most potent cortisol releasers of the macronutrients. So the more protein you eat, the more cortisol release you trigger.[2] Scientists have now uncovered the pathways used by proteins to induce cortisol secretion, and they've figured out how to block them. It's easy to do. You just block your alpha-1 adrenergic receptors. "That's great!" I hear you say. But don't get too excited yet. Giving alpha-1 blockers to humans before a protein meal blunts cortisol release, but it also blunts protein absorption. The sad-but-true fact is that you need cortisol in order to assimilate your dietary proteins properly. It's also a fact that the protein-induced cortisol rise is very short, unlike stress-induced cortisol secretions.

increases its cortisol production until the blocking properties of RU486 are overwhelmed.

Many attribute the potent muscle-building effects of anabolic steroids to their so-called ability to block cortisol receptors. That's unlikely to be true, however, as most studies have failed to demonstrate a connection between androgens and cortisol receptors. Some "enhanced" bodybuilders are able to pack on muscle mass even though their cortisol secretion is very high. Furthermore, no studies have noted ultrarapid cortisol elevation after subjects took anabolic steroids, as could be expected with any effective cortisol-receptor blocker.

Bodybuilders didn't stop with RU486 in their quest to suppress cortisol. They moved on to drugs that can stop natural cortisol production. With a very low cortisol level, they expected fast muscle growth. What they didn't expect were the strange allergies that some of them experienced.

Bertil Fox.

Bertil Fox.

Cortisol as an anti-inflammatory hormone

Not all the effects of cortisol are bad. Some are even helpful to bodybuilders. Weight training induces various degrees of trauma to the muscle fibers, damage that triggers some inflammatory reactions. The more severe the trauma, the more serious the inflammation, which will cause the body to manufacture more of such harmful substances as tumor necrosis factor (TNF). The muscles have TNF receptors, and when a TNF molecule activates a receptor, it activates the ubiquitin/proteasome catabolic pathway.[3] In other words, TNF has an almost direct catabolic effect on muscle cells. Cortisol can inhibit the TNF secretion due to an inflammation, which means that cortisol possesses both catabolic and anticatabolic properties. If you suppress cortisol release, your body will manufacture more TNF and the catabolic effect of cortisol will be unopposed.

CONTROLLING CORTISOL SECRETION

Your goal is not to inhibit normal cortisol secretion but to *control* its secretion and effects. Some drug users have found a radical way of controlling their cortisol secretion: they take synthetic cortisol, and the exogenous glucocorticoids strongly inhibit their natural cortisol secretion. Instead of having fluctuating cortisol levels, they establish an artificial baseline.

It's tricky, but some people have made their best gains while using this method. Of course, if you make a mistake with your dosages, don't expect to pack on muscle. What's more, the technique won't work for natural bodybuilders. Drug users can artificially control their protein turnover rate, a feat natural bodybuilders can't accomplish. We're limited to methods of cortisol control that are more natural but not as precise.

Using a preworkout testosterone booster can moderate the cortisol response to exercise. Testosterone can't completely prevent cortisol's effects, but it can lessen its response to stress.

Growth hormone boosters have the same property. GH can oppose an excessive elevation of cortisol. So can phosphatidylserine (PS). None of the supplements eliminate the stress-induced cortisol elevation; they just keep it within reasonable limits. On the other hand, they don't suppress the basal cortisol release, so they don't cause problems.

Jonathan Lawson.

Jonathan Lawson.

CONTROLLING CORTISOL'S EFFECTS

Using both a GH booster and a testosterone booster offers another advantage. Cortisol tends to depress GH, IGF-1, and testosterone secretions, but the natural boosters fight those effects. The carb-drink-induced elevation of insulin also tempers some of the harmful effects of cortisol. For example, insulin is one of the few hormones that can combat the cortisol-induced elevation of the ubiquitin/proteasome proteolytic pathway.

In addition, cortisol stimulates the manufacture and release of glutamine, which empties the muscles' glutamine reserves. Glutamine can be formed from other muscle

Rich Piana.

Besides stress, there are other ways in which workouts elevate cortisol. If the workout is long, your blood glucose level is likely to fall, leading to hypoglycemia, which triggers cortisol secretion. Taking a carb drink absorbed during training will prevent the fall of blood glucose, countering the hypoglycemia. It can also maintain insulin at a high level, which, as you'll see, is important.

If you choose to fight the exercise-induced cortisol rise, I strongly suggest you use a natural anti-inflammatory supplement, such as omega-3s, a group of essential fatty acids derived from fish oil. The omega-3 fatty acids have been shown to inhibit the elevation of catabolic substances such as inflammation-induced TNF.

amino acids, thanks to an enzyme called *glutamine synthetase*. Whenever the enzyme activity is stimulated, the muscles start to lose their amino acids. The bottom line is, when muscle glutamine levels are low, anabolism is reduced.

Cortisol increases the expression of glutamine synthetase from the muscles. By taking oral glutamine, you blunt that effect, as glutamine represses the enzyme's activity.

I cannot stress enough the importance of glutamine. When muscle glutamine is low— for example, because cortisol is high—the activity of the glutamine synthetase goes into action, which leads to a vicious circle. Cortisol reduces muscle glutamine a little, but a lowerthan-normal muscle glutamine level automatically triggers even more glutamine synthetase expression, which in turn further reduces muscle glutamine levels.

Of course, in the very short run glutamine synthetase *increases* muscle glutamine levels; however, the newly formed glutamine is rapidly exported from the muscles. In theory, glutamine is very effective at putting an end to the vicious circle. In practice, the entry of the glutamine from the blood into the muscles is not as important as we might hope. Consequently, taking oral glutamine reduces only *some* of the wasting effects of cortisol, although in theory it can potentially blunt them completely.

Muscle branched-chain amino acid (BCAA) reserves are also negatively affected by cortisol, which increases the activity of another muscle enzyme called branched-chain keto dehydrogenase (BCKAD). The effects of BCKAD are very different from those of glutamine synthetase. While the latter manufactures glutamine, BCKAD destroys BCAAS. And while glutamine tames glutamine synthetase activity, BCAAS activate BCKAD.

The rationale for using oral BCAAS is that cortisol reduces muscle-BCAA levels. Even if a portion of the oral BCAAS is wasted because it activates BCKAD, another portion replaces the cortisol-induced loss of BCAAS. So, unlike what happens with glutamine, the oral BCAAS don't directly combat cortisol's wasting effects. Rather, they repair some of the damage it causes.

Aaron Baker.

Craig Titus.

Roger Applewhite.

USING CORTISOL'S EFFECTS

Although high cortisol levels tend to waste muscle mass, studies have demonstrated that the muscles play catch-up when cortisol levels return to normal. A day of rest acts as a brake on the ramped-up cortisol production, making it a powerful anabolic inducer. The lack of stress creates an anabolic overshoot. You need to take regular rest days to ensure muscle growth.

The schedule in the table in the next column creates a dynamic control of cortisol levels, along with selective inhibition of its wasting effects, with phosphatidylserine, GH, and testosterone boosters. For natural bodybuilders it's a blueprint for relieving one of the major obstacles to impressive muscle mass.

Mass-Building, Cortisol-Control Supplement Schedule

6 A.M. (30 minutes before breakfast)

Testosterone boosters, such as 19-norandrostedione (100 milligrams) and tribulus terrestris (500 to 1,000 milligrams).

Reason: Testosterone boosters have been shown to help reduce cortisol levels, creating a more anabolic environment; they may produce better effects when taken on an empty stomach.

6:30 A.M. (breakfast)

Protein and carbs (for example, skim milk, oatmeal, egg whites).

Protein powder, 2 scoops in water.

L-glutamine, 2–3 grams.

Reason: To reverse the catabolic overnight fast and replenish glutamine, which cortisol escorts out of muscle tissue.

9:30 A.M.

Protein drink or unsweetened low-fat yogurt.

Reason: To aid optimal growth and recovery.

11:30 A.M.

Testosterone booster, such as 19-norandrostenediol (100 milligrams).

Reason: Testosterone boosters have been shown to help reduce cortisol levels, creating a more anabolic environment; they may produce better effects when taken on an empty stomach.

Noon (lunch)

Protein and carbs (for example, baked chicken and mixed vegetables).

Reason: To aid optimal growth and recovery.

3 P.M.

Protein drink or low-fat cottage cheese or unsweetened, low-fat yogurt.

Reason: To aid optimal growth and recovery.

Ronald Coleman.

Mass-Building, Cortisol-Control Supplement Schedule (continued)

3:30 P.M.

Cortisol antagonist, such as Cort-Bloc (600 to 800 milligrams; 3–4 scoops).

Reason: To control cortisol secretion during your workout.

Testosterone boosters, such as 5-androstenediol (50 milligrams) and tribulus terrestris (500 to 1,000 milligrams).

Reason: Testosterone boosters, 5-androstenediol especially, can help control cortisol.

Creatine monohydrate, such as Creatine Stak (5 grams).

Reason: muscle volume and anaerobic energy.

4 P.M. (during training)

Slightly diluted fruit juice sipped during the workout.

Reason: Keeping insulin levels high helps blunt the cortisol release caused by training.

5:30 P.M. (immediately after training)

Protein powder, 3 scoops in 12 ounces of orange juice.

Creatine monohydrate, such as Creatine Stak, 2–3 grams.

L-glutamine, 2–3 grams.

Reason: This mixture boosts insulin, which helps blunt cortisol release and forces amino acids, such as the all-important L-glutamine, and creatine into the muscle cells while the muscle structures are primed.

7 P.M. (dinner)

Protein and low-glycemic carbs (for example, tuna and broccoli).

Reason: To aid optimal growth and recovery.

Cortisol antagonist, such as Cort-Bloc (600 to 800 milligrams; 3–4 scoops).

Reason: To control cortisol so you get a stronger GH surge from your booster before bed.

10:30 P.M.

GH Stak.

Reason: Growth hormone boosters can oppose the anticatabolic effects of cortisol as well as enhance muscle growth, fat burning, and connective tissue repair. Don't eat any food for three hours prior to ingestion.

References

1. Naman, N. 1995. Effets d'un anti-glucocorticoide sur la proteolyse musculaire induite par une brulure. *Ann Endo.* 56:83.
2. Reznik, Y. 1993. L'appétit vient en mangeant, le cortisol aussi. *Presse Med.* 22:407.
3. Reid, M. B. 1998. Skeletal muscle myocytes undergo protein loss and NF-kB activation in response to TNF-alpha. *Faseb J.* 12(suppl):A471.

Bruce Patterson.

Chapter 15

MUSCLE-PACKING NUTRITIONAL SOLUTIONS FOR HARD GAINERS

BY SIMON HALFORD

You've been trying to get bigger. You've been training like an animal and watching what you eat, but you're still frustrated—it's just not happening. Sure, you're tipping the scale with a few more pounds, but you're not exactly ready for the cover of *Ironman*. You're frustrated because you've been doing everything you're supposed to do to get big, right? So what's going wrong? A quick review of some basic weight-gain principles can't hurt.

To pack on lean mass in a short period of time, you must not only train correctly—heavy weights with low-to-medium reps in a routine that's primarily made up of compound exercises like squats and rows—but also eat enough of the right things and supplement food intelligently. Let's focus on eating and supplementing for maximum weight gain in the shortest time possible.

There are three cardinal rules of nutrition for maximizing your gains:

1. Consume more calories than you burn on a daily basis.
2. Consume enough protein.
3. Eat frequently and don't skip meals, especially postworkout meals.

BUMP UP THE CALORIES

The key to muscle growth is maintaining an anabolic state in your body. Anabolic refers to being in a positive balance for growth. For bodybuilders, that positive balance means gaining more muscle than your body is breaking down naturally through exercise and stress. The opposite of an anabolic state is a catabolic one, in which there is a negative balance for growth. Without an adequate supply of calories, your body enters a catabolic panic state. It begins to feed off itself by using nutrients from its own tissues, including muscle.

To avoid that undesirable catabolic condition, you must consume an adequate number of calories. Depending on your metabolism and activity level, the calories you need may vary. One guideline that holds true for everyone, however, is this: You must consume more

Porter Cottrell.

calories than you burn every day to quickly achieve your weight-gain goals.

To illustrate the role calories play in gaining weight, think of your body as a savings account. Every time you take in calories, you're making a deposit; every time you exercise and expend calories, you're making a withdrawal. Also keep in mind that your body makes withdrawals throughout the day just to stay alive. If you want to get rich or gain weight, you'd have to deposit more calories than you withdraw each day. That's simple enough. So how many calories do you need to gain mass?

A good rule of thumb is to take in about 15 to 20 times your bodyweight in calories, depending on your metabolism. For example, if you weigh 200 pounds, you should eat at least 3,000 and up to 4,000 calories per day. Of those calories, approximately 60 percent should come from complex carbohydrates, 30 percent from high-quality proteins, and about 10 percent from fat.

Porter Cottrell.

A great way to make sure you meet the guidelines without having to do a great deal of math is to load half of your plate with foods rich in complex carbohydrates (like potatoes, rice, pasta, and yams) and fill the other half of the plate with a high-quality lean protein (like skinless chicken breast, turkey breast, or tuna). The fat has a way of taking care of itself. Although most people don't have any trouble getting their daily intake of carbohydrates or fats, protein is another matter entirely.

High protein: A must for growth

A growing number of studies are confirming what bodybuilders have claimed all along: bodybuilders need more protein—a lot more.[1,2] Even in conventional scientific circles the experts now agree that strength athletes and bodybuilders take in about 1.8 grams of protein per kilogram of bodyweight a day.[3] That's a whopping 225 percent of the current RDA.

To ensure getting adequate protein, many hard-training bodybuilders consume at least 1 to 1.5 grams of protein for every pound of bodyweight. To use the previous example, if you weigh 200 pounds, your protein quota would be at least 200 to 300 grams a day.

As a bodybuilder you need that extra protein primarily for the repair and growth of muscle tissue. Without sufficient protein your body shifts from an anabolic state to a catabolic one as it starts tearing down muscle tissue to meet its metabolic needs. Maintaining a diet rich in high-quality protein helps prevent the shift to that undesirable catabolic state, so be sure to consume plenty of whey protein, egg whites, chicken breast, turkey breast, and lean fish such as tuna, halibut, and orange roughy. To fully benefit from a high-calorie, high-protein diet, however, you must also eat frequently.

Meal frequency

Every successful bodybuilder—from amateur to Olympic contender—eats at least six times per day. Successful bodybuilders know that by eating so frequently, they provide their muscles with a steady stream of nutrients to keep

Dave Tuttle.

them in an anabolic environment. Eating six times per day—every two to three hours—not only helps maintain an anabolic balance but also prevents your body from dipping into its own muscle tissue to get nutrients like protein. That undesirable cannibalizing effect can occur because the body can't store protein the way it does fats or carbohydrates. In other words, your body must have protein as it needs it or it will dip into muscle tissue, which is metabolically active, to get protein. For that reason alone it's critical to provide your body with protein and other nutrients throughout the day. And at no other time is it more critical to get those nutrients than after a workout.

Dave Tuttle.

Are carbohydrates the only nutrient you need following a workout? Contrary to what many people believe, you also need protein and a little bit of fat to maximize muscular gains. Now, more than ever, science is proving the importance of a properly balanced post-workout meal.

Several researchers at the recent 44th Annual Meeting of the American College of Sports Medicine presented results of their studies of consuming postworkout meals with different combinations of macronutrients. They found that by eating a combination of carbohydrates, protein, and some fat right after exercise, subjects got the best results in terms of replenishing muscle glycogen, increasing protein synthesis, and decreasing protein catabolism.[4]

If you're like most hard-training athletes, you sometimes feel nauseated right after an intense workout. Food is the last thing on your mind. That's understandable, but you still need carbs, protein, fat, and other nutrients for your body. The ideal way to get them into your body quickly is to use a nutritional supplement drink.

Will Willis and Karen Koumas.

Postworkout meal

To avoid the cannibalizing, you always want to avoid skipping meals. If you're going to miss one, however, make sure it's not your post-workout meal! Immediately following a strenuous workout, you have a window of opportunity to give your body the nutrients it craves. For instance, because your glycogen stores are usually depleted after a workout, your body tends to absorb a large amount of carbohydrates to replace the lost glycogen. Therefore, high-carbohydrate meals have less of a tendency to be converted to bodyfat after a workout.

Chris Faildo.

Of the thousands of different supplements on the market, none better satisfies the body's postworkout needs than a weight gainer. That's because a weight gainer packs lots of protein, carbs, and other nutrients into your body. The main problem with most weight gainers is that they're also loaded with simple sugars and lactose, which make them fat gainers or, at best, difficult to digest. The ultimate solution is to consume a weight gainer that provides everything your body needs *without any of the fillers* like sugars, saturated fats, and hard-to-digest lactose.

THE QUEST FOR THE PERFECT POSTWORKOUT SUPPLEMENT

What would be the formula for the best postworkout meal? For starters, it would contain about 150 grams of complex carbohydrates like maltodextrin or polydextrose, that are slowly absorbed to replenish glycogen levels. It would also contain 30 grams of a superprotein.

What do I mean by a *superprotein*? One rich in proteins that support muscle growth while promoting fat metabolism. Can any one protein deliver all of that? Maybe. Different protein sources yield different benefits. The goal is to combine only those components of the best proteins so that you end up with the best of all possible worlds. Let's look at three proteins with unique characteristics that when combined could very well produce the world's ultimate superprotein: whey, casein, and soy.

Whey protein

Whey protein has the highest biological value (BV) of any protein in existence. In fact, the body absorbs whey protein 60 percent better than the next most absorbable protein source, whole eggs.[5]

Porter Cottrell.

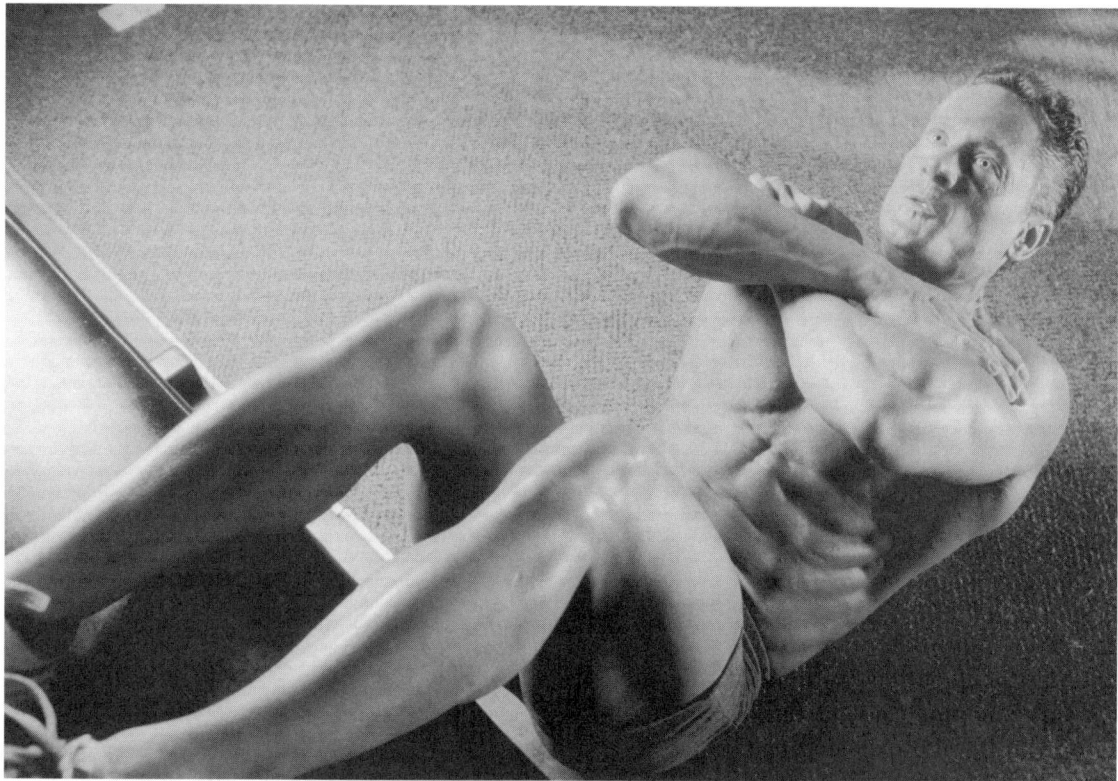

Dave Tuttle.

While it's true that whey is a superior source of protein because of its high bioavailability, few people are aware of whey's additional benefits and immune-system-enhancing properties. For example, whey protein is rich in whey peptides, a special group of amino acids that are absorbed and retained better than whole proteins or free-form amino acids. They offer you some excellent benefits.[6] For instance, the dipeptides and tripeptides of whey signal the liver to produce somatomedin-C, the anabolic growth factor that stimulates muscle growth.[7]

Whey protein also contains high levels of the branched-chain amino acids (BCAAS), leucine, isoleucine, and valine. The BCAAS are important to all bodybuilders because they help insure against loss of muscle size and strength.[7] In addition, whey protein can help your immune system stay strong and healthy. Recent studies show that it contains special types of antibodies called *immunoglobulins*, which play a specific role in the immune system: they can attack foreign substances that

enter the body. So it appears that they help the immune system do its job more effectively.[8] A strong immune system is essential so that your body can focus on important duties such as recovering from your last workout.

While whey protein is an excellent start to the formula, you'd be selling yourself short if you didn't include one other milk protein—casein.

Arne List.

Chris Faildo.

Casein

Casein, the other milk protein, is often thought to be inferior to whey, since it has a much lower biological value. Casein has a BV of 77, while whey can score as high as 159. When it comes to bioavailability, there's no contest—whey is king. Many people, however, don't know that casein has unique properties that even whey can't match.

One such strength lies in casein's tendency to form a gel in the intestinal tract that's responsible for slowing the transit time of nutrients through the intestines. The slowing of transit time can exert a time-release effect on proteins and other nutrients, thereby giving the body more time to fully digest and absorb them. Additionally, casein is extremely high in the amino acid glutamine; in fact, it contains 21 percent glutamine peptides, making it a better source of glutamine than an egg or even whey protein. Glutamine is classified as a conditionally essential amino acid, but as a body-

builder you'd be advised to consume it under any condition.

Here are some interesting facts about glutamine:

- Glutamine accounts for about 60 percent of all free amino acids in the body.[8]
- It can be used by the body as a fuel, for a new body protein, and to make other important compounds and amino acids.[8]
- There are especially high concentrations of glutamine in muscle cells.
- If you don't eat enough glutamine-rich foods, your body tears down muscle tissue to get what it needs.[8]
- Recent studies show that supplemental glutamine, even at just a few grams per day, prevents muscle breakdown.[8,9]

Mike O'Hearn.

Jean-Pierre Fux.

As you might imagine, the blend of whey and casein in the hypothetical ideal postworkout formula delivers some impressive nutrients to help you pack on muscle. Even so, that powerful combo can be further improved upon. Enter soy.

Soy

Soy—the stepchild of the protein world—is the only protein missing from the superprotein formula. Before you frown in utter disbelief, you should know that soy protein has recently been validated by the scientific community as having benefits of interest to bodybuilders. The latest studies prove conclusively that soy protein has metabolism-stimulating properties.[10]

Craig Titus.

It stimulates the metabolism by enhancing the body's production of the thyroid hormone thyroxine (T_4), a key regulator of metabolic rate. Usually, the more thyroxine your body produces, the faster your metabolism. That unique characteristic makes soy protein very desirable. Think of the possibilities: a revved-up metabolism can help minimize the risk that the extra calories you've consumed in your weight-gaining quest will be deposited as bodyfat. For that reason alone soy is a must. It's also comforting to know that, with respect to amino acids, soy protein nicely complements whey protein and casein.

Because soy is high in several of the key amino acids found in whey protein and casein, it increases their potency. Specifically, soy is rich in the "critical cluster" of amino acids[11] that consists of glutamine, the branched-chain amino acids, and arginine. You already know the benefits of glutamine and the BCAAS. Arginine, however, has a trait that few people were aware of until just recently. Many compelling clinical studies done with humans have found that arginine plays a key role in stimulating the release of muscle-forming anabolic hormones, including human growth hormone.[12] Is there any doubt that arginine belongs in this formula?

Booster nutrients

The perfect weight-gain formula wouldn't be complete without the presence of those nutrients responsible for assisting the organs and tissues that work with the muscles. The most important among such nutrients are essential fatty acids, vitamins, and minerals.

You definitely want your hypothetical formula to be low in fat—5 grams per serving at the most—but still contain the fatty acids that the tissues need to function optimally. The use of medium-chain triglycerides in the form of MCT oil is the answer. MCT molecules are unique because the body burns them preferentially, the way it prefers carbohydrates instead of fats.

For fats, carbohydrates, and proteins to be assimilated properly, the body needs a combination of vitamins and minerals to aid in their

Arne List.

absorption. Ideally, you want a full spectrum of vitamins and minerals in the formula. You also want an enzyme blend as extra insurance that all of the nutrients are digested completely. It would include the following enzymes:

- Alpha amylase and malt diastase to help digest carbohydrates.
- Protease to help digest the whey protein, casein, and soy protein.
- Lactase to help digest any traces of the milk sugar lactose found in the milk proteins.

In a perfect world one formula would contain all of those enzymes and other nutrients, but nature didn't provide complete meals designed to help you build huge muscles. It should come as no surprise, however, that some scientific experts are already mixing their own unrefined versions of the superprotein. Mackie Shilstone, the clinical director of Louisiana State University's Medical Center and a well-known trainer of professional athletes, made it known in a recent interview that a whey, casein, and soy combo would be the "ultimate in protein supplementation." He continued by stating, "I mix whey and soy proteins together as a meal replacement and use casein peptides following my workouts."

Another well-respected authority, world-champion powerlifter and certified Medical Review Officer Mauro Di Pasquale, M.D., recently praised the protein blend: "Although a high-quality whey protein offers tremendous benefits to athletes, one can't deny the benefits and utility of the other protein powders." Like Mackie, Mauro claims to use a similar blend. "I use a combination of soy, casein, and whey protein that I make up myself from three different products, each one containing one of the protein isolates in a quality form," he said.

Sure, those scientists and trainers have access to the isolated ingredients, but what about the rest of us? Is the answer to run to the grocery store and buy a shopping cart filled with milk, tofu, and cottage cheese? That would never work because we'd be getting only traces of the good stuff and too much of the fattening, stomach-bloating stuff,

such as sodium, lactose, and saturated fat. We can't escape the fact that we actually need the miracle of modern food-processing technology to ensure a formula rich in desirable characteristics while low in particular other characteristics.

All right, I admit it: I'm a supplement junkie. I love to try new supplements that look promising. No, I don't run out and purchase something because of marketing hype; I look beyond the typical marketing BS and try to get a feel as to whether a new product makes sense. If it does, I try it. I've always got better results when I supplemented my food intake with high-quality bodybuilding products. Until now, weight gainers were a category of supplements that I'd totally written off.

Like most bodybuilders, I thought of weight gainers as, well, weight gainers. They weren't too exciting, just an old standby type of supplement that I used a lot in my early

Karl List.

Bertil Fox.

Ofer Samra.

tional weight gainers and brainwashed everyone, including me, into thinking that they were all useless.

The danger in subscribing to generalizations is that sometimes something really good comes along and you miss it. While I haven't changed my opinion of weight gainers entirely, I have become more open-minded since finding one that meets all the criteria for postworkout nutrition. I've been using this particular product for about a month now, and I can say that it really hits the spot as the perfect postworkout meal.

The product I'm referring to is the new Kwik Size XXXL from Labrada Bodybuilding Nutrition. It's a super low-sugar weight gainer (4 percent sugar, compared with 56 percent for the average weight-gain product) and it's low in fat and sodium. On the other hand, it's high in the superprotein combination of whey, casein, and soy, and it's fortified with digestive enzymes (Labrada calls it "Peptigen") and vitamins. All in all, the company has done a great job with this formula. It's nutritionally sound, tastes wonderful (even my girlfriend likes it), and in my opinion is definitely worth trying, especially if you're a hard gainer.

Don't let Labrada's colorful Kwik Size ads fool you; this is a serious weight gainer with a new twist designed with the hard gainer in mind. Even though it's labeled a "low-sugar weight gainer," I think of it as a nutritionally dense postworkout meal that gives me just the right amount of calories, protein, and nutrients. I feel fuller and stronger on Kwik Size, and so far I haven't gained any fat around my midsection, which is a first.

Remember, to maximize gains you must consume more calories than you burn on a daily basis, get enough of the right protein, and eat frequently. If you don't approach your nutritional program as seriously as you approach your training, you're destined to plateau out, and your muscle gains will come to a halt.

With proper training, nutrition, and supplementation, you'll be on your way to making that sweetest of all bodybuilding rewards—big muscle gains!

days in the gym, when I didn't care what kind of weight I gained. Just about every single weight gainer I used in the past was loaded with sugars, such as dextrose or fructose. While that makes for a great taste, sugar isn't the best thing to be consuming if you're anything like me and tend to put on unwanted fat. My feelings were echoed in the popular bodybuilding press, which ripped apart conven-

References

1. Lemon, P. W. 1996. Is increased dietary protein necessary or beneficial for individuals with a physically active lifestyle? *Nut. Rev.* 54:s169–s175.

2. Lemon, P. W. 1991. Effect of exercise on protein requirements. *J Sports Sci.* 9:53–70.

3. Tarnopolsky, M.A., et al. 1992. Evaluation of protein requirements for trained strength athletes. *J App Phys.* 73:1986–1995.

4. Wojcik, J. R., et al. 1997. Effect of postexercise macronutrient intake on metabolic response to eccentric resistance exercise. *Med Sci Sports Exercise.* 29 (Suppl.5):S294.

5. Renner, E. 1983. *Milk and Dairy Products in Human Nutrition.* Munich, Germany: Volkswirtschafticher Verlag.

6. Poullain, M. G., et al. 1989. Effect of whey proteins, their oligopeptide hydrolysates, and free amino acid mixtures on growth and nitrogen retention in fed and starved rats. *J Par Enter Nut.* 13:382–386.

7. Colgan, M. 1993. *Optimum Sports Nutrition.* New York: Advanced Research Press.

8. Ehrlich, N., and J. Shabert. 1994. *The Ultimate Nutrient: Glutamine.* Garden City Park, NY: Avery Publishing Group. 14,15,20,58.

9. Welbourne, T. C. 1997. Enteral glutamine spares endogenous glutamine in chronic acidosis. *J Par Enter Nut.* 17:23S.

10. Stroescul, V., et al. 1996. Metabolic and hormonal responses in elite female gymnasts undergoing strenuous training and supplementation with Supro Brand isolated soy protein. Brussels, Belgium: Second International Symposium on the Role of Soy in Preventing and Treating Chronic Disease.

11. Protein Technologies International. 1997. *Total amount of critical cluster of amino acids in protein sources.* St. Louis, Missouri: Ralston-Purina Research. Chart 1/97.

12. Masuda, A., et al. 1990. Insulin-induced hypoglycemia, L-dopa, and arginine stimulate GH secretion through different mechanisms in man. *Regulatory Peptides.* 31:53.

Chapter 16

FOOD:
THE ULTIMATE DRUG

BY ELLINGTON DARDEN, PH.D.

What kind of perverse, sadistic game is nature playing with us?

In our times technology has presumably created almost perfect foods—low in fat and high in calories, yet also high in flavor. Why, then, are most of us struggling with expanding waistlines and poorly defined muscles?

What if there was something simple you could do that would help you stay lean, muscular—and healthy—for the rest of your life with little effort or expense? Something that didn't involve any far-fetched and impossible-to-follow diets? What if it turned out that much of your bodyfat is, in fact, a *result* of your eating low- or nonfat foods—or even drinking fruit juices? It's true.

Eating certain types of foods, in the right combinations, can initiate profound changes in your body. Food is the ultimate drug. Many of the top nutritionists in the world, including Dr. Barry Sears, author of the bestseller *The Zone*, have recently reached this conclusion.

Let me preface the remainder of this chapter by saying that there's no inherently bad type of food. Proteins, fats, and carbohydrates are all essential, and avoiding any one of them for a long time is a nutritional death wish. The bad, almost criminal, thing is what some food manufacturers have done to one food group: carbohydrates.

A LITTLE SCIENCE

All carbohydrates, from a teaspoon of honey to a slice of homemade bread, are simple sugars. Insulin is a hormone produced by the body that controls levels of sugar in the bloodstream. When you eat any form of sugar, your body releases insulin to handle it. There are a couple of places it can go. First of all, insulin can drive some of the sugar, known as glucose, into muscle cells. The trouble is that the muscle cells can hold only so much sugar, and the extra, through a complex series of chemical reactions, is converted into fat and stored around your waist, your thighs, or any other place it finds convenient. To make matters

worse, insulin has a vasodilatory effect, which enables it to deliver fat to fat storage sites efficiently.

As you might guess, certain foods elicit a bigger insulin release than others, and that's something diabetics have known for a long time. In fact, diabetics use a little tool called the glycemic index, or GI, to help them figure out what foods they can eat. The GI of a food indicates its ability to raise your blood sugar level, and it's expressed as a percentage of the response to an equivalent amount of a standard food: white bread.

White bread has a GI rating of 100, as does sucrose, a type of sugar. Foods that have a high GI are assigned values of about 20 to 40. If you don't want to raise insulin levels (and we'll get into why you wouldn't want to), you should try to avoid eating foods that have a high GI.

Of course, it isn't all that simple. There are a lot of things that influence a food's GI. Fat is one of those things. Fat actually slows the absorption of a food, thus eliciting less of an insulin release. About 80 years ago a scientist discovered that bread with butter raised blood sugar a lot less than plain bread.[1] Therefore, if you take the fat out of a food, it elicits a larger blood sugar response, thereby causing insulin levels to soar. Insulin, then, drives more fat into fat storage tissue, which in turn causes your waistline to grow.

A HIGHLY PROCESSED PROBLEM

Ironically, our whole country is in the grip of a fat-free craze. Many food manufacturers have ripped the fat out of cookies, ice cream, cakes, breads, chips, you name it, in an effort to provide you with diet-conscious, nonfattening foods. Of course, by removing all the fat, they inadvertently created foods that are more hazardous to your waistline than the foods they replaced!

There's another problem with many of today's foods: they're highly processed. Generally, the more you process a food, the smaller the particles of starch become. If you ingest small particles of starch, they're absorbed very quickly, which causes the body to release a large amount of insulin.[2] Years ago, before modern milling techniques, people ate bread that contained large pieces of coarse grains and seeds. That's an important point when you consider that the incidence of dia-

Bruce Patterson.

betes, a disease characterized by inefficient insulin release or the body's inability to use the insulin it does release, started to climb phenomenally with the introduction of new milling equipment about 300 years ago.[1]

Until the early 1990s it was actually thought that replacing starch in food with sugar would make the GI even worse. That's proved to be incorrect. Many of today's foods are so highly processed that adding sugar to breakfast cereals, in lieu of starch, actually decreases the GI.[3] Likewise, other studies have found little or no difference between the blood sugar response of cookies made with or without sugars. It seems sugar has gotten a reputation it clearly doesn't deserve.

So the fact of the matter is that in creating fat-free or reduced-fat foods manufacturers have created foods that are absorbed into the bloodstream very quickly, where they cause the body to release a large amount of insulin. The result—over days, months, and years—is a huge storehouse of fat.

Doing too good a job

When you eat high-GI foods, they cause your body to produce large amounts of insulin. The insulin disposes of the sugar in your bloodstream all right, but sometimes it does too good a job. In fact, the insulin often overshoots

Katy Rickman.

the mark, resulting in a lower-than-desired blood sugar level, known as *hypoglycemia*, that sends a message to your brain to go out and get a snack.

In other words, eating high-GI carbs stimulates the appetite, causing you to hit the vending machines long before lunchtime. That behavior, over time, results in a body that weighs about as much as a vending machine.

A hormonal nightmare

Insulin, if managed correctly, is anabolic.[4] In small amounts, released at the proper times, it can help you put on muscle. Unfortunately, because of our modern-day eating habits, most people suffer from an overabundance of insulin, which can lead to a condition called insulin resistance.

Insulin resistance is common in the United States, and millions of people suffer from it to some degree. There's also a lot of evidence to suggest that an overabundance of insulin—as you might find in someone who eats high-GI carbs all the time—eventually makes you "immune" to its effects. What happens is that, for whatever reason, insulin is no longer as effective as it used to be. Insulin has to bind to receptors on cells before it can do its job, and those receptors either degrade, lessen in number, or just don't show the same affinity for insulin anymore.

Insulin resistance isn't good. If insulin can't do its work, another hormone that works in opposition to insulin gets free rein. The other hormone, glucagon, actually tears down body tissues to give the body the energy it needs to function, and sometimes those tissues include muscle. Even if you're not actually producing enough glucagon to tear down muscle tissue, you might well be producing enough to make it harder to put on new muscle.

Furthermore, excess glucagon can lead to feelings of sluggishness and contribute to atherosclerosis, known as hardening of the arteries. It can also develop into full-blown, insulin-dependent diabetes.

Insulin resistance can cause other hormonal problems as well. Research indicates that there's an association between insulin and testosterone. Generally speaking, obese people—who are typically insulin-resistant—have lower testosterone levels.[5] Something about an insulin-resistant body causes testosterone levels to drop, and how can you build muscle when your testosterone is low?

High insulin levels have also been implicated in decreased serum levels of DHEA (dehydroepiandrosterone) and DHEAS (dehydroepiandrosterone-sulfate).[6,7] That, in fact, may well be one of the reasons that high insulin levels cause hardening of the arteries, since DHEA and DHEAS seem to exert cardioprotective actions.

High amounts of insulin also counteract the effects of growth hormone.[7] Too much insulin, and you have too little GH—too little, that is, to benefit from the hormone's growth-promoting effects.

Dave Palumbo.

Mike O'Hearn.

1. An overabundance of insulin drives calories into storage as fat.
2. An overabundance of insulin can cause a hypoglycemic, or low blood sugar, crash, causing you to be very hungry a lot sooner than you might have been otherwise.
3. Insulin counters the effects of GH, and of the two, you'd much rather have high levels of GH.
4. An overabundance of insulin can lead to a condition known as insulin resistance, which can lead to hardening of the arteries, sluggishness, and possibly insulin-dependent diabetes. Insulin resistance can cause decreased levels of testosterone, DHEA, and DHEAS. It can also lead to increased levels of glucagon, a catabolic hormone that might actually metabolize muscle tissue, or at least make it harder to put on muscle.

Mia Finnegan.

Typically, it's thought that insulin resistance is something that happens as you get older. Maybe, maybe not. Many experts now believe that eating foods with a high GI for a long enough time can lead to insulin resistance.

Experiments with rats have shown that when you feed them high-GI foods for nine weeks, they develop insulin resistance. When given injections of a type of sugar, the rats had to secrete twice as much insulin as normal rats to clear the sugar from their bloodstreams. Conversely, the insulin resistance did not get worse in rats fed a low-GI diet.

A brief recap

Here's a review of how having chronically high insulin levels—from eating high-level GI foods—can be bad for you:

Jonathan Lawson.

PUTTING THE DATA TO THE TEST

With all this talk about glycemic indices and blood sugar levels, you may wonder how these measurements are taken. It's quite easy, actually, as any diabetic will tell you. Most drugstores sell devices called glucometers, and they're used to let diabetics know how long it'll be before they need another injection of insulin. To test your blood sugar levels, you simply need to calibrate the machine, poke yourself in the finger hard enough to produce a drop of blood, place the drop on a special strip of paper, and then feed the paper into the glucometer. Within seconds you get a reading that equates to your blood sugar levels at the moment the drop of blood was produced.

Under ideal circumstances you want your blood sugar levels to stay under 100 milligrams per deciliter of blood. In healthy human beings the blood sugar levels hover around 70 to 85 milligrams. Any food eaten will cause a rise in blood sugar within a few minutes. In normal people it will peak in about half an hour, and, depending on how much food you eat—and its GI, of course—it will drop to normal again within an hour or two.

Again under ideal circumstances you want any food you eat to produce a gentle sloping curve, with the blood sugar not really going much higher than 100. If you could eat that way pretty much day in and day out, you'd probably never develop insulin resistance, you'd feel more energetic, and you'd likely have the same waist you did when you were much younger.

Unfortunately, most foods don't elicit an ideal blood sugar response. Take a look at the blood sugar response to a bowl of Cheerios cereal (about 100 grams) with skim milk. Cheerios aren't usually considered a calorie-filled indulgence. In fact, some people might even think of them as a diet food. They are, however, a highly processed cereal, and they contain very little fat—both of which contribute to a high GI.

My subject's fasting blood sugar level was 83. Fifteen minutes after he ate a bowl of Cheerios, it was 118. After 30 minutes it was 141. It dropped back to a subpar 71 after an hour. The insulin surge prompted by the high blood sugar was apparently so large that it overshot the mark, bringing his blood sugar down to a level that was much lower than his normal, fasting blood sugar. So he felt hungry by that time. His body was telling him to eat again so he could raise his blood sugar levels back to normal.

Other foods, like rice cakes, fat-free crackers, and even apple juice have essentially the same effects. It's not hard to guess that both the cereal and the fat-free crackers are highly processed—their tiny starch particles are digested quickly and race into the bloodstream. Maybe you're puzzled by the apple juice, though. Obviously, it's not a processed wheat or grain product; however, apple juice, despite being made largely of fructose, a low-GI sugar, is a highly processed food. The pulp has been squeezed and broken down, so it enters the bloodstream quickly.

Curtis Leffler.

What about a food that isn't processed much at all, like oatmeal? Fifteen minutes after he ate a bowl of oatmeal, my subject's blood sugar rose from a fasting level of 79 to 96. After 30 minutes it was only 91, and after 60 minutes it had decreased to 79, right where we started.

The oatmeal drove blood sugar up ever so slightly, and it reverted to baseline after an hour. Glycemically, oatmeal is a pretty good food. The trouble is that you can't live on oatmeal. For one thing it doesn't contain enough proteins, fats, or vitamins and micronutrients to live on. For another it tastes like, well, oatmeal.

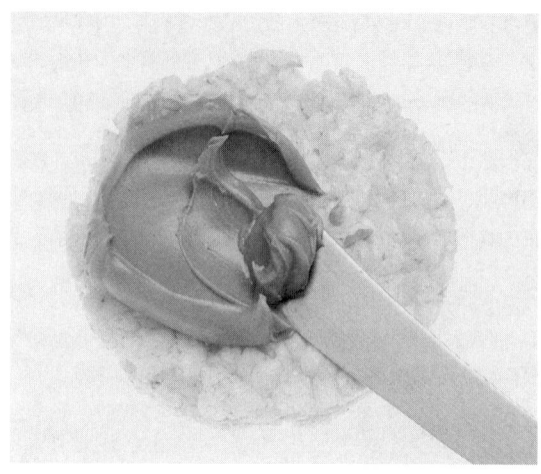

SHOULD YOU GIVE UP YOUR FAVORITE FOODS?

By now, you're probably thinking I'm going to advocate some sort of extreme diet on which you subsist entirely on oatmeal and some other drab-tasting low-GI foods. Nothing could be further from my mind. There's a solution to the high-GI, high-insulin, high-fat-on-your-body problem, and it's fairly simple. There are, however, a few rules to follow.

1. When eating processed foods, be careful of those that have a high GI. Look for ones that are stone-ground and that have whole seeds visible. For example, European-type whole-grain breads are fine, as are products like oatmeal, lentils, or brown rice. Similarly, when eating pasta products, try to choose those that are made from whole grains. Examples of highly processed common foods to avoid are many children's breakfast cereals, conventional white-flour-based pastas, and nonfat crackers.

2. If you must eat highly processed carbohydrates, eat them in combination with proteins or fats. As mentioned above, if you eat a rice cake or saltine, put a dab of peanut butter—the kind that's made with peanuts, salt, and nothing else—on it. If you have to have a bowl of Special K in the morning, eat it in combination with a protein dish, such as scrambled egg whites.

3. Along the same lines, don't snack on fruit or fruit juices by themselves. Have them in conjunction with some other food that contains proteins, unprocessed grains, or some healthy fats, such as monosaturated canola and olive oils or peanut butter, or essential fats such as those found in fish oils.

By combining a potentially high-GI food with a little fat or protein, or by mixing it with unprocessed, whole-grain foods, you can keep the insulin response down to acceptable levels and avoid all the excess baggage that comes with perpetually high insulin levels. That means you can keep your appetite in check and avoid binge eating at the vending machines.

Of course, it all sounds easier than it might be in practice. Combining foods takes thought, and there are many variables when it comes to guessing the insulin-raising capabilities of a particular food or dish. For instance, a boiled new potato has a low-GI rating, but when you bake it, the GI rises significantly. It seems that the baking makes the starch molecules more digestible. Many other foods are in the same boat. It would take some sort of glycemic-index specialist to get it absolutely correct. Nevertheless, you can make a significant impact by following these three rules of eating.

References

1. Horowitz, J., et al. 1993. Metabolic responses to preexercise meals containing various carbohydrates and fat. *Am J Clin Nutr.* 58:235–241.

2. Brand-Miller, J., and K. Foster-Powell. 1995. International tables of glycemic index. *Am J Clin Nutr.* 62:871S-893S.

3. Surwit, R. S. 1997. Metabolic and behavioral effects of a high-sucrose diet during weight loss. *Am J Clin Nutr.* 65:908–915.

4. Tessari, P. 1994. Effects of insulin on whole-body and regional amino acid metabolism. *Diabetes/Metabol Rev.* 10:253–285.5.

5. Pasquali, R., et al. 1997. Effects of acute hyper-insulinemia on testosterone serum concentrations in adult obese and normal-weight men. *Metabol.* 46:526–529.

6. Lavalle, P., et al. 1997. Effects of insulin on serum levels of dehydroepiandrosterone metabolites in men. *Clin Endocrin.* 46:93–100.

7. Polderman, K. H., et al. 1996. Effects of physiological and supraphysiological doses of insulin on adrenal androgen levels. *Horm Metab Res.* 28:152–155.

Dr. Daniel Gwartney.

Chapter 17

EFFERVESCENT CREATINE

BY DANIEL GWARTNEY, M.D.

Competitive and recreational athletes use creatine monohydrate for its performance-enhancing, or ergogenic, properties. It's been shown in numerous studies to be beneficial in activities that depend on the anaerobic energy system, which include such sports as powerlifting, sprinting, swimming, and field events. Such sports typically involve high-intensity, short-duration movements with short rest breaks during training. The energy for them comes primarily from ATP stored in skeletal muscle and ATP regenerated from phosphocreatine stores. Anaerobic glycolysis is another potential energy source, though its relatively slow rate of ATP production prevents it from contributing to short-duration activities (that is, those of less than 30 seconds).

Studies show that oral creatine supplementation increases total muscle creatine stores. Increases in creatine and phosphocreatine have been demonstrated by muscle biopsy, and those results correlate well with studies that measure anaerobic work performance.

To date, there have been no serious adverse effects associated with creatine supple-mentation; however, an undetermined percentage of creatine users has reported stomach upset, diarrhea, and cramping, which suggest poor intestinal absorption. Anecdotal reports of muscle and tendon injuries appear to be related to inappropriate training and supervision during the initial period of creatine supplementation. Athletes may be susceptible to overtraining, or they may develop or exacerbate an imbalance between muscle groups during periods of accelerated strength and performance improvements.

Creatine monohydrate is typically found in powder form, and manufacturer directions recommend consuming it in 8 to 16 ounces of water, juice, or isotonic sport drinks. They also recommend a loading phase at the beginning of a creatine cycle that consists of four to six 5-gram servings a day for four to six days. A maintenance phase then follows, with the recommended dose being 5 to 20 grams a day. There are some deviations from the recommendations, but there's little evidence to support alternative modes of creatine use.

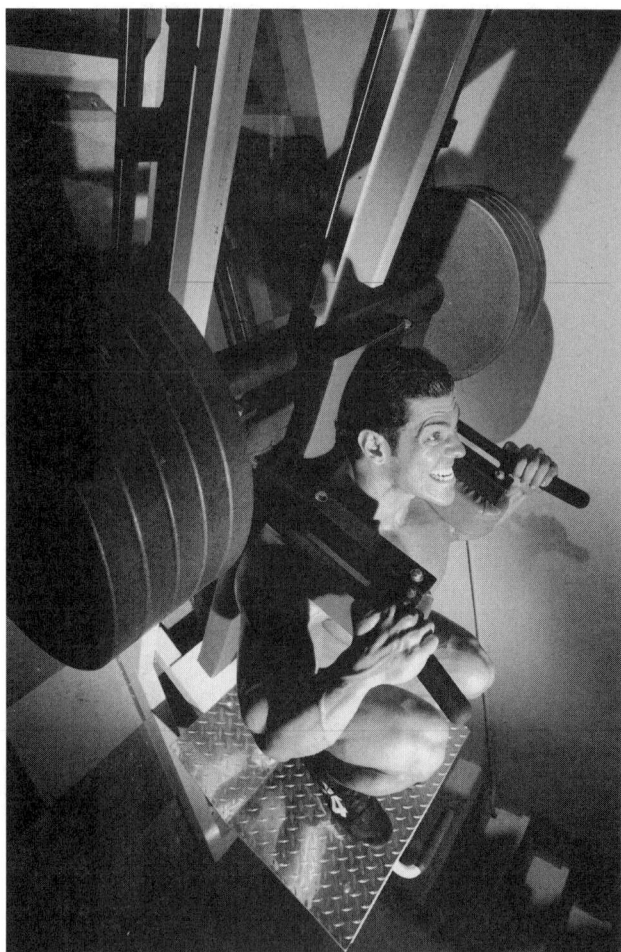

Rich Piana.

The majority of problems associated with creatine monohydrate occur during the loading phase. People complain of poor intestinal tolerance, as evidenced by cramps or diarrhea. Commonly, their drinking more fluids resolves the complaints, which are rarely mentioned during the maintenance phase.

There are numerous creatine monohydrate products around. A beneficial one combines creatine and high-glycemic carbohydrates. Studies have shown that creatine uptake into muscle is enhanced in the presence of insulin with those products, which leads to increased muscle creatine stores over what subjects got with straight-creatine supplementation. There are other formula additions to creatine, but none have shown to add much benefit. One possible exception is inorganic phosphate salts, which may aid in maintaining the creatine-to-phosphocreatine ratio in the muscle cells.

Adding carbohydrates has improved the ergogenic value of creatine; however, there's still a barrier keeping people from realizing the complete ergogenic value of creatine. That barrier is the poor intestinal absorption. Creatine uptake is mediated by an active sodium-dependent transporter, and there's extremely little passive absorption of creatine in the intestine, due to the substance's poor solubility in water and the ionic nature of the intestinal environment. Compounding the problem is the supposed down-regulation of the creatine transporter that occurs during supplementation. The absorption problem has been clearly demonstrated even during the relatively short loading period. That's consistent with the findings regarding other guanine compounds, such as taurine, in which the intestinal receptor is shown to down-regulate following oral supplementation.

Overcoming that barrier should effect a significant improvement in creatine's ergogenic profile, in both the acute loading phase and the maintenance phase. Before the introduction of effervescent delivery, that just wasn't possible. The only recourse was to bypass the oral delivery route in favor of intravenous administration. While there may be a place for that in therapeutic environments—for example, where there are patients with certain mitochondrial conditions—it's an unacceptable option for athletic enhancement or recreational use.

Effervescence occurs when weak acids and bases are combined to create a buffered solution at a stable pH. It typically involves the use of bicarbonate salts, which form carbon dioxide gas upon activation. The appearance of the carbon dioxide gas gives the bubbling, or fizzing, effect that you get with popular over-the-counter remedies for indigestion and allergy.

Effervescence is a useful and applicable delivery device for creatine for many reasons. First, and possibly most important, is the buffering effect. Stabilizing the pH of the creatine-containing solution at the pI, or isoelectric point, promotes an electrically

Rich Piana.

Jennifer Goodwin.

Bruce Patterson.

Jim Quinn.

balanced, or neutral, creatine molecule known as a *zwitterion*. The net electrical charge of the zwitterion is zero. Creatine is a small molecule, so it's now theoretically available for passive absorption—in addition to the active transport that has been shown to down-regulate. That's important for two reasons. It provides an alternate and less restrictive means of accessing the mesenteric venous system—the transport system can be quickly saturated even during the initial dose. Second, it allows for continued absorption, even during the maintenance phase.

An additional benefit of the buffering is the so-called dumping effect. Creatine is of maximum benefit at select times of the day: in the morning after the nighttime fast, for instance, or right after training. These windows of opportunity are short. Studies suggest that a 200-milliliter volume is held in the stomach for 40 minutes to one hour. If you drink more or have consumed a meal high in fat or protein, that period may extend for

Ofer Samra.

Arne List.

hours. The problem is, very little absorption takes place in the stomach by design.

The stomach's role is mostly to grind up and break down the food by acid digestion. Its mucosal lining is nearly impermeable, which protects it from the destructive effect of the stomach acids.

The duodenum and the remainder of the small intestine are the sites of greatest absorption. The effervescent delivery of creatine causes a pH shift in the stomach, which the body senses as a signal to dump the stomach contents into the duodenum. Once the creatine passes into the duodenum, the greater surface area and absorptive function of the intestinal lining quickly absorb the creatine zwitterions. What's more, the creatine transporters are located in the jejunum and ileum, two other sections of the small intestine.

Alex Marenco.

Craig Titus.

As the effervescently delivered creatine is almost completely absorbed, you don't have the stomach problems inherent in creatine use. Noneffervescently delivered creatine, particularly after transporter down-regulation, is typically passed down the small intestine, drawing water into the lumen of the bowel in an attempt to dilute and dissolve the crystals. The creatine crystals act as an irritant and have a high osmotic pull. Unfortunately, the majority of water transfer takes place in the large intestine, which has very little absorptive capacity. That leaves the creatine in the colon, along with the attendant water load, and it's the water efflux and the presence of the colonic creatine that lead to diarrhea, cramps, and dehydration. The greater absorption with effervescent delivery should remove that curse.

Bruce Patterson.

the supplement's effects on repetitive sprints, isotonic, isometric, or timed-recovery resistance training than on marathon running or long-distance cycling.

One study that's been done in the exercise science laboratory is the measure of anaerobic work performed on a cycle ergometer. That measures maximal energy output, which depends on ATP and the phosphocreatine shuttle. The study showed an increase in anaerobic work performance (AWP) of 10 percent following a creatine-loading phase. Adding carbohydrates increased the AWP to 20 percent over the control group. That was the standard by which creatine products were gauged for the past three years—that is, until effervescent creatine with carbohydrate showed a significant improvement in AWP to 30 percent over the control subjects.

Craig Titus.

Bear in mind that creatine is designed to augment anaerobic work performance. That means a muscle working to near maximal exertion is highly dependent on the amount of ATP available during the period of exertion. Long-distance races and exercise with low-intensity loads aren't significantly affected by creatine supplementation. Therefore, in terms of research, it's more appropriate to measure

Craig Titus.

Marketing groups present the findings— and the figures—in confusing terms. Here are the basic facts shown by the research:

- Creatine provides a positive ergogenic effect when used and measured correctly.
- The addition of a high-glycemic carbohydrate enhances the muscle uptake of creatine.
- Thyroid hormone and vitamin E also seem to play roles in the muscle uptake of creatine.
- Creatine's greatest drawbacks are its ionic nature and osmotic pull. Creatine's effects are further impeded by the use of active transport and the supposed down-regulation of intestinal creatine receptors.
- Transit time may cause a variable delay in creatine delivery to the intestine for absorption.
- Effervescent delivery buffers creatine at its pI, which allows it to exist as a zwitterion.
- Effervescence also decreases transit time, providing a quicker and more reliable delivery to the intestine.
- Creatine as a zwitterion may be available for both active and passive transport, bypassing the reduced availability from receptor downgrading.
- Creatine causes a 10 percent increase over the AWP of control subjects.
- Creatine with carbohydrate causes a 20 percent increase over the AWP of control subjects; that is, it's twice as effective.
- Effervescently delivered creatine with carbohydrate causes a 30 percent increase over the AWP of control subjects; that is, it's three times, or 300 percent, as effective—and 150 percent as effective as creatine and carbohydrate.

One further benefit of the effervescent creatine is that it is dose-metered in the individual packages, which means that each ingredient is added to each package individually to ensure that each serving contains the amount of each ingredient it's supposed to contain. That contrasts with the large tubs of batched products, like the creatine-and-carbohydrate blends. The mixing process in those is imprecise, and settling occurs during both manufacturing and shipping. Creatine may be nearly nonexistent in one portion of the batch and over the stated amount in another. The effervescent system also requires a foil-sealed pack, which provides for a longer shelf life and fewer storage-related changes, and the individual serving packs make it more convenient to use.

Effervescent creatine represents a novel and effective use of a pharmaceutical delivery system that enhances the positive benefits of creatine and negates the adverse effects.

Don Long.

Chapter 18

LEGAL STACK
THE ANDROGEN HORMONES ANDROSTENEDIONE AND ANDROSTENEDIOL

BY MICHAEL MOONEY

New bodybuilding supplements come and go, but once in a while one passes the test of time. Do you remember the short-lived popularity of inconsequential substances like "similax" and beta "ectazone"? You can count on your fingers the supplements that have staying power, the ones that people loyally continue to buy. Well, the new legal androgen hormone androstenediol and its predecessor androstenedione appear to be up to the test.

I first learned about androstenedione (A-dione) when my friend Patrick Arnold, the chemist for LPJ Research who rediscovered this molecule, asked if I knew someone who could translate German data on it. I recommended my research partner, Jim Brockman, so Jim and I were the first to see the data Pat had collected on what has become the year's most popular new bodybuilding supplement, Androstene 50, which is produced by Osmo. Even though the information on A-dione looked very good, I was quite skeptical as to whether it would perform as well as the data suggested if taken orally. Even so, I tried it,

and it produced the characteristic testosterone effect on neurotransmitters right away. Sex has never been better.

Since A-dione's potential effectiveness made biochemical sense and it worked well for me, I began to recommend it to the HIV patients I work with. I suggested that they experiment with it during the refractory period of depressed testosterone production they experience after they come off an anabolic steroid cycle. Many of those guys typically experience greatly decreased energy, libido, and mood, and they quickly lose muscle tissue, so they feel terrible.

One of my hardest refractory cases is a guy named Joe, who is HIV-positive and has AIDS. Joe's natural production of testosterone after he comes off steroids is so poor that he barely has the energy to leave his house to go to the store. Although Joe should remain on a perpetual replacement dose of testosterone, his response to testosterone cypionate injections diminishes greatly if he doesn't take a short break every six months or so.

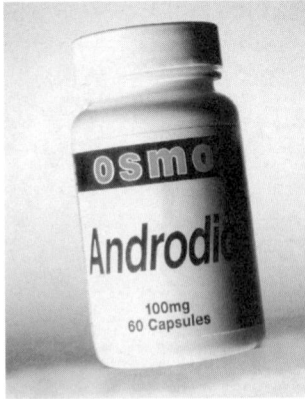

Joe called me during a recent break to tell me that he'd started using A-dione (in the form of Osmo's Simply Androstene), and his energy level and libido had increased so much that he actually felt human again. I was happy that my recommendation seemed to work, but I still hadn't seen lab tests that proved this wasn't a placebo effect, and I felt a bit guilty that I was recommending something to critically ill people that hadn't actually been quantified with lab work. The only data on androstenedione so far have come from a European study done with women—who respond differently than men—and the data published in the German patent that Jim had translated. (Unfortunately, patent data are usually highly questionable.)

So I spent my own money for some blood tests on myself. I used two capsules of Simply Androstene. Each capsule contains 50 milligrams of androstenedione, with 200 milligrams of rice bran solubles (RBS) and 3 milligrams of zinc. It's like the better-known Osmo product Androstene 50, except it contains no lysophosphatidyl choline (LPC). Also note that while there are a number of androstene products on the market, I used the Osmo product because I have seen lab analyses that confirm it is full-potency androstenedione. Tests done on one person can't be considered conclusive, but I just wanted to find out whether there was actually anything happening to testosterone metabolism. After going through a couple of rounds of tests, I'm sure that there is.

Don Long.

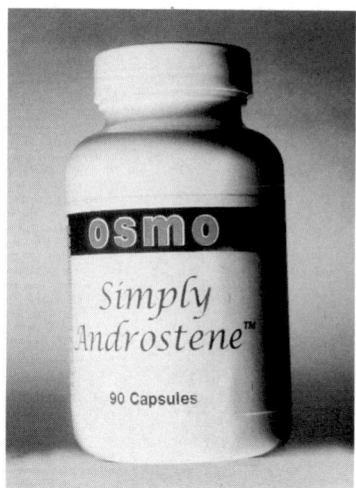

MY BLOOD TEST

With my stomach empty, I had blood drawn at baseline before I took the A-dione and then again at one and two hours afterward. The tests produced some surprises. Based on the limited available data on A-dione, I expected to see a quick increase in testosterone of several hundred percent, but that isn't what happened. Instead, I learned that the RBS appear to alter the release pattern of the androstenedione, causing it to release considerably more slowly than it would all by itself. Consequently, it takes longer to alter testosterone activity in the body. In fact, the test showed that two capsules of Simply Androstene, which delivered 100 milligrams of androstenedione, didn't actually cause a significant response after one hour.

After two hours, however, the free testosterone had increased by 63 percent over baseline, and the total testosterone had increased by 47 percent. So it seems that Simply Androstene takes longer to produce an effect than pure A-dione should, and the release is probably sustained a lot longer than with pure A-dione as well.

Because I had no idea that the time-release phenomenon would happen, I stopped the lab tests after two hours. It would be interesting to see whether there's still something going on at, say, six hours. From what people tell me about their response to these RBS-containing products, I suspect that the release is drawn out about six to eight hours. This effect might be useful if you wanted to create a sustained testosterone release as a foundation for another product that produces quick testosterone spikes, like the newest member of the androstene family, pure androstenediol. Remember that the next time you think about putting together an effective stack to increase testosterone for building muscle.

I should also note that *Muscle Media* recently published the results of lab tests done with A-dione that weren't as impressive as my experience. The subjects in those tests experienced a peak increase in total testosterone of only about 24 percent. (The researchers didn't measure free testosterone.) With those results being so different from mine and showing a lot less improvement in total testosterone, it's obvious that this subject needs a lot more testing done before any conclusions can be reached—other than the idea that there really is an increase in testosterone activity.

Jason Arntz.

THE NEW KID ON THE BLOCK: ANDROSTENEDIOL

About a year after Pat got me interested in A-dione, he called to talk about his newest discovery, 4-androstenediol (A-diol), to be sold as Androdiol (at present Osmo and GEN have the exclusive rights to this supplement). Pat had uncovered data showing that A-diol converted to testosterone much more efficiently than A-dione and via a different enzyme (3-hydroxysteroid dehydrogenase for A-diol and 17-beta hydroxysteroid dehydrogenase for A-dione), so he figured that it should beat the pants off A-dione and perhaps work additively with it (since they each require different enzymes and probably wouldn't compete for the enzymes).

Pat's chemistry is generally good, and his argument was interesting. I asked him to send me a sample of pure A-diol—without any RBS or other ingredients—so that I could test it. The tests were completed in late August, and this time I spread the measurements out a little more, with the first blood drawn at 30 minutes and the last done at two and a half hours.

Sure enough, although the timing of the tests was different, I did get an indication that Androdiol may be an improvement over A-dione. I want to underscore the point that since A-diol and A-dione utilize different enzymes, theoretically, they might work very well together. That's the reason I call it an androgen stack. Such a dual-enzyme, androgen-pathway stack would logically produce interesting effects on testosterone levels, possibly more than either could do alone. Wouldn't it be worthwhile to conduct blind blood tests on this combo with a significant number of subjects?

As for the results I got with my A-diol experiments, 30 minutes after I took 100 milligrams, my total testosterone was up 62 percent. After one and a half hours it was up 37 percent, and at two and a half hours it still was up 21 percent.

My level of free testosterone was even more impressive, as it more than doubled and was up 114 percent at 30 minutes. It dropped to 57 percent at one and a half hours and was still at 57 percent after two and a half hours. Now, that can be considered a significant spike.

ANDROSTENE OUTTAKES

I also did blood tests with 100 milligrams of pure androstenedione on a 29-year-old male and got an increase in free testosterone of 346 percent at 30 minutes that stayed about 300 percent during the two hours that I measured it, but with no change in total testosterone. I was amazed, to say the least. When we sat down to figure out what had happened, however, Jim remembered that raising insulin can decrease sex-hormone binding globulin (SHBG) significantly,[1] which would cause an

Danny Hester.

Alex Marenco.

increase in free testosterone. Our subject had taken the A-dione with a sugary drink that increases insulin.

If the rise in insulin was the cause of the radical rise in free testosterone, my suggestion would be to take your androstene stack with a sugary, insulin-raising quick-release drink like grape juice—perhaps at the same time you take your creatine. The drink should have no fat and no protein so that it gets into the bloodstream quickly. You may notice a much better effect, especially on brain chemistry factors like libido and aggression.

There are obviously a lot of ways to look at the metabolism of the androstene molecules. I wish I had an unlimited budget to do comprehensive tests on these compounds.

EXACTLY WHAT IS FREE TESTOSTERONE?

Total testosterone is an interesting factor, but free testosterone gives us more to go on because it's the subset of blood testosterone that is immediately ready to diffuse into the cells and impart testosterone's butt-kicking message. Free testosterone, which makes up about 2 percent of the body's total testosterone, at one time was thought to be the only part of the testosterone that was active in the body. Now many in the scientific community opine that there is important activity involving some of the bound testosterone as well.

While the SHBG-bound testosterone—which makes up about half the "bound" part of the total testosterone—is unavailable for use at any given time, the other half of the bound testosterone appears to be a bit more readily available. This almost-free testosterone is primarily bound to a blood protein called albumin. Since its binding to albumin is weaker than the binding of testosterone to SHBG, it can release from the binding proteins and diffuse into cells in its free state more readily than can the SHBG-bound testosterone—although not as easily as the free testosterone.[2]

The key point about free testosterone, compared with total testosterone, is that the effects in the brain are largely mediated by the free testosterone. That means a quick rise in free testosterone will probably cause neurotransmitter changes that will more quickly make you feel more aggressive, more energetic, and more sexual.[3] The question is whether it will also have an effect on muscle growth. It might, if it is employed correctly.

Laura Bass.

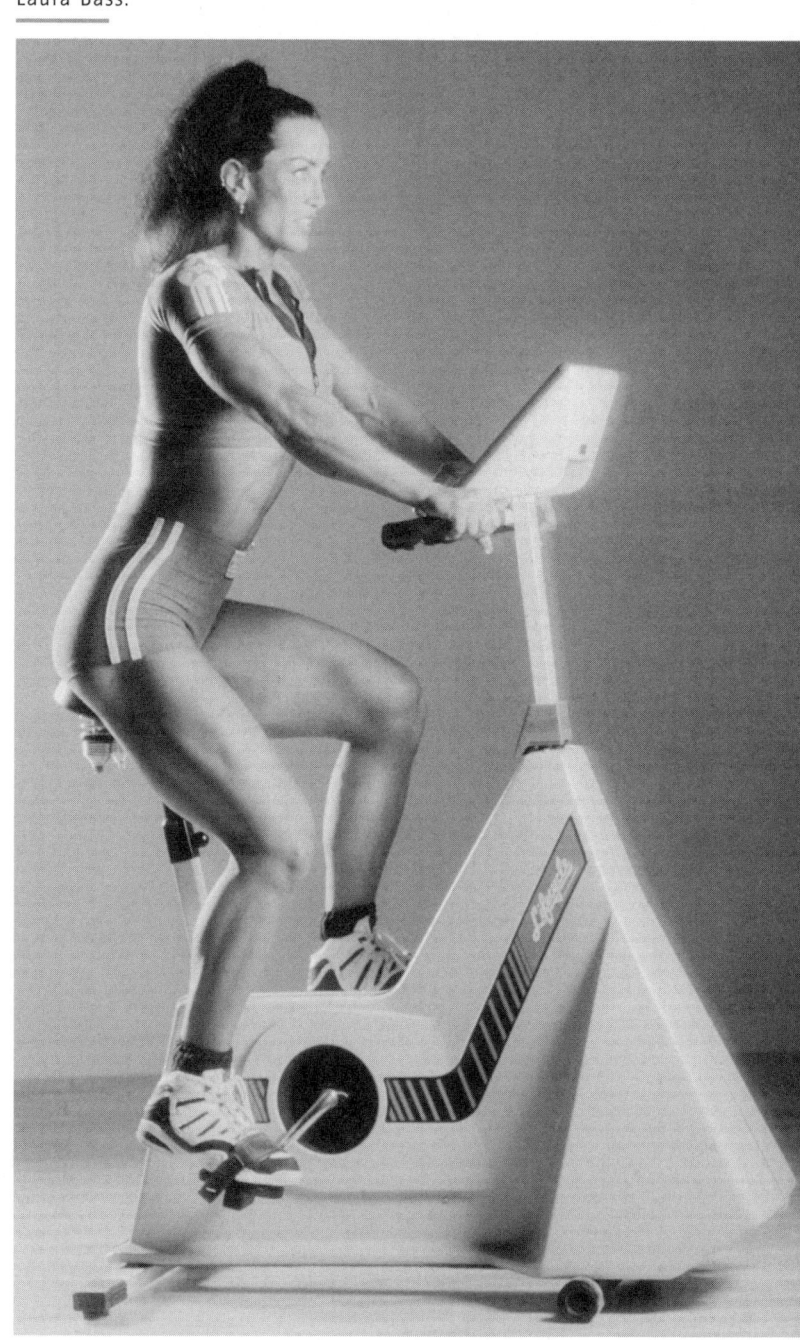

Gregory Reid.

Note that while the effects of testosterone in the brain can occur in minutes,[4] the anabolic effect takes place as a succession of events over several days. So, in order to increase anabolism by using such supplements as the androstenes, you would have to create significant periods of increased testosterone activity over a long term. That's where the stacking of supplements (for example, the two products discussed earlier) several times per day comes in.

Simply producing a good spike in the body's active testosterone levels can have a quick effect on brain centers that are involved with sexuality and drive, but to get the effect to work on your muscles, you'll want to create a net average increase in testosterone activity that is present most of the time. What's more, producing spikes in testosterone production at specific times, like before workouts, might improve the net anabolic effect in the same way as does taking in lots of calories during the few hours after lifting weights. Logically, you want to have plenty of testosterone present when the greatest training stimulus occurs. You might also use this kind of spike to decrease the possibility of catabolism caused by the fall in testosterone and increase in cortisol that can take place toward the end of a long, hard workout.

HOW TO STACK THEM

Creating a muscle-building androstene stack would include initiating a sustained increase in testosterone several times a day by taking 100 milligrams of androstenedione first thing in the morning and again in the midafternoon or a couple of hours before training, depending on when you train. Then, to create quick peaks for specific activities, combine 50 to 100 milligrams of androstenedione with 100 milligrams of androstenediol. You can use this combo a half hour before a workout to give you extra aggressiveness and maybe again at the end of the workout to help decrease the potential for catabolism. Take the second one with a sugary drink like grape juice to raise your insulin and jack up your free testosterone.

The introduction of androstenediol brings another interesting period of experimenting with natural bodybuilding supplementation. Who'd ever have thought there'd be legal natural steroids!

References

1. Strain, G., et al. 1994. The relationship between serum levels of insulin and sex hormone-binding globulin in men: The effect of weight loss. *J Clin Endocrinol Metab.* 79(4):1173–1176.

2. Isselbacher, Karl J. 1994. *Harrison's Principles of Internal Medicine.* 13th ed. McGraw-Hill.

3. Simpkins, J. W., et al. 1983. Variable effects of testosterone on dopamine activity in several microdissected regions in the preoptic area and medial basal hypothalamus. *Endocrinology.* 112(2): 665–669.

4. Wehling, M. 1995. Looking beyond the dogma of genomic steroid action: Insights and facts of the 1990s. *J Mol Med.* 73(9):439–447.

Jonathan Lawson.

Chapter 19

STOP PARATHYROID HORMONE FROM KEEPING YOU SMALL

BY MICHAEL GÜNDILL

All the hormones that your body produces naturally have an effect on your appearance, musculature, strength, percentage of bodyfat, and other factors. Some have positive actions, while others have negative effects. As a natural bodybuilder your goal is always to optimize the secretion of the former while reducing the release of the latter.

Unfortunately, the distinction between positive and negative hormones isn't always obvious. Some so-called negative hormones may have significant beneficial effects, and it isn't always possible to naturally influence your hormonal secretions as much as you'd like. Parathyroid hormone (PTH) is one of the hormones you should consider as a bodybuilder. PTH is clearly *negative* as far as building muscle is concerned. However, it's relatively easy to reduce the secretion of it naturally.

The parathyroid hormone is responsible for regulating calcium in the body. As its name indicates, PTH is secreted by the parathyroid glands, which are found at the base of the neck, just to the side of the thyroid. PTH is secreted when the level of calcium in the blood is lowered. At a low dose it increases bone density, but at high doses—and if its secretion becomes chronic—PTH attacks your bones and makes them more fragile.

THE RESEARCH TRAIL

Four scientific studies, which we will discuss, are interesting because they show that taking the minerals calcium and magnesium increases lean muscle mass rapidly. That fact came to light only by chance in the first study.

Physicians specializing in sports medicine tried increasing the calcium intake of college basketball players.[1] Their objective was to see if calcium supplements would increase bone density. Research had already shown that intense physical activity can increase bone density, especially during the growth period of adolescence. On the other hand, athletic activity also increases losses of calcium, particularly

Jonathan Lawson.

through perspiration. It can, therefore, create a calcium deficiency just when the body most needs the mineral. Yet the researchers noted that 2 grams of calcium a day increased not only bone density but also muscle mass. In other words, physical exercise plus calcium supplementation increases muscle mass significantly more than does exercise alone.

The second study involved magnesium supplementation during a seven-week period of weight training.[2] The subjects taking magnesium supplements gained more strength than those who followed the same weight-lifting program but received a placebo. The researchers speculated that the gain was due to an increased rate of muscle protein synthesis.

The third study demonstrated that a total intake of magnesium above 7 milligrams per kilo of bodyweight led to substantially higher strength gains in trained football players than did a lesser intake.[3] The fourth study, which was performed on bodybuilders in Germany, demonstrated that intense training depletes magnesium stores. A magnesium supplement not only prevented the loss, but it also promoted anabolism.[4]

What's the relationship between muscle gains facilitated by calcium supplementation and those induced by magnesium supplementation? There's at least one. The two minerals lower the secretion of PTH.

HOW DOES PTH RELATE TO MUSCLE?

There is calcium in your muscles. It's stored at the periphery of your muscle fibers in reserves called the sarcoplasmic reticulum. It is freed from those reserves by a nervous stimulation signaling your muscles to contract, as calcium induces the contraction of muscle fibers. The more calcium is freed, the more strongly your muscles will contract. Therefore, calcium is your ally during exercise.

After training, however, the muscle microtrauma induced by the workout—especially the negative parts of the movements—causes cal-

Jim Shiebler.

cium leaks. Microfissures in your muscle fibers permit calcium to leave its reserves and spill into the muscles. Since calcium is toxic for the damaged muscle fibers, that translates into soreness and an intense muscular catabolism.

Parathyroid hormone and calcium in the muscles

When the level of calcium in the blood—not the muscle—is lowered due to an insufficient intake or excessive losses of it through sweat and urine, the parathyroid glands produce PTH. The purpose is to draw calcium from the reserves in order to restore calcium levels in the blood. Since your muscles contain some calcium, the PTH recruits it by forcing it to leave its reserves, which enhances the passive basal calcium leak into the muscles.

PTH performs its harmful work by stimulating a proteolytic factor called calpains. The muscles naturally contain calpains in a dor-

mant state. Once activated by training-induced calcium leaks, calpains literally cut part of the muscle fibers. What's worse, they also digest the so-called easily releasable myofilaments, transforming your hard-earned muscles into simple amino acids. By activating calpains, PTH therefore has a traininglike effect on your already traumatized fibers.

That's a catastrophe for bodybuilders, as it reinforces the catabolic effects of exercise without having any positive effects; that is, stimulation of anabolism. PTH distances you from your objectives: to optimize the positive aspects of training while reducing its negative impacts.

The wasting effect of PTH is well illustrated in maladies in which the secretion of parathyroid hormone is too high. People suffering from hyperparathyroidism—who have too much PTH—rapidly lose muscle mass, suffer from fatigue, and have trouble recuperating. Doesn't that sound like overtraining?

That brings us to the question, Why would a bodybuilder have an above-average PTH secretion?

Steve Cuevas.

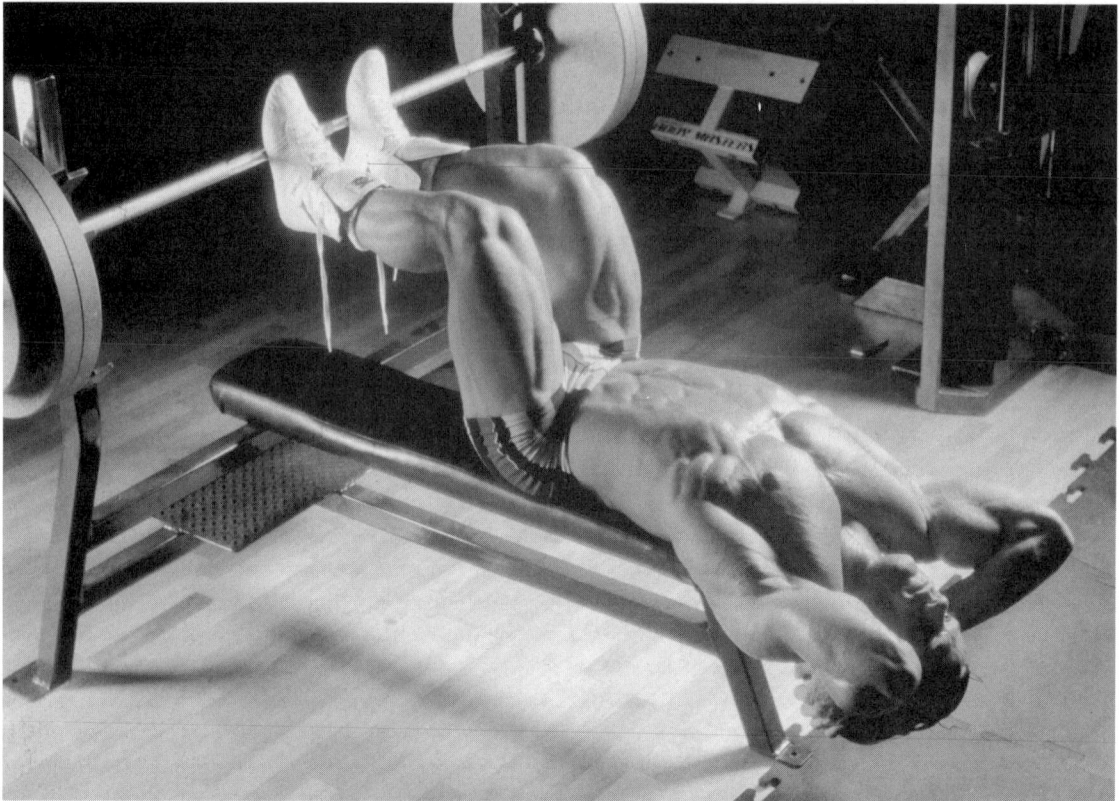

Jason Arntz.

PARATHYROID HORMONE SECRETION AND TRAINING

Bodybuilders talk a lot about the harmful effects of cortisol, a catabolic hormone whose secretion increases following training. If parathyroid hormone is so harmful and if its secretion increases after training, why do bodybuilders neglect it?

The reason is simple. Until the early 1990s, all the research done on athletes showed that the PTH secretion wasn't affected by physical training. No elevation of PTH meant no PTH-induced catabolism and, therefore, no problem. At the beginning of the 1990s, however, new measuring techniques appeared that were much more sensitive and reliable, and scientists discovered that the physical training typical of bodybuilders significantly increases the secretion of PTH. Research has demonstrated that a very small amount of strength training is enough to induce the release of an impressive amount of

PTH.[5] So parathyroid hormone really does pose a problem.

As if leaching amino acids—especially glutamine—from the muscles wasn't bad enough, PTH has other harmful effects in bodybuilders. First of all, an elevation of parathyroid hormone causes a rise in the production of cortisol. Parathyroid hormone also reduces the effects of insulin on the muscles, thereby lessening its anticatabolic and anabolic effects. Furthermore, PTH-induced insulin resistance causes greater difficulties in replenishing muscle glycogen, and so it delays recuperation. An increased PTH secretion also reduces the levels of red blood cells while preventing the kidneys from making erythropoietin (EPO, a hormone that makes red blood cells). In other words, too much PTH will tend to make you anemic. All in all, parathyroid hormone has a very negative balance sheet.

Its only positive aspect might be its impact on adipose tissue. In a test tube parathyroid hormone accelerates fat loss. Unfortunately, in

Curtis Leffler.

reality many people who suffer from hyper-parathyroidism not only have less muscle but are also fatter than average. That may be explained by the insulin resistance that PTH induces.

Parathyroid hormone and creatine

As mentioned, bodybuilders normally talk about creatine only in terms of getting it inside their muscles and the best way to load the muscles with it. We know that by increasing

insulin levels, we can cause more creatine to be transported into the muscles. Nevertheless, that might not be the whole story. If some hormones help to transport creatine, others should reduce its transport. If some hormones, like testosterone, build up creatine levels in the muscles, others should deplete the muscles of it. PTH has both of those negative effects.

Several mechanisms are involved. PTH-induced insulin resistance in the muscles will reduce the entry of creatine, and PTH will waste away the creatine found inside the muscles. It both slows entry of new creatine and depletes what's already there. So if you don't do something about your above-average PTH secretion, you may not get the most out of your creatine supplement. You will recover more slowly and have smaller, weaker muscles and a higher bodyfat level.

The anti-PTH effects of magnesium may spare muscle creatine—which explains, at least in part, the strength gains associated with high magnesium intake.[2,3,4]

Parathyroid hormone and testosterone

Some people are especially susceptible to an increase in the PTH level. For example, that's the case with people who use androgenic prohormones. Also, bodybuilders who take substances such as clenbuterol, mahuang, and caffeine, which activate beta adrenoceptors, will have an increased secretion of parathyroid hormone. The situation is exacerbated by a low-calorie diet, which also tends to increase the secretion of PTH.

Therefore, it's essential for bodybuilders to prevent the rise of parathyroid hormone. That's especially true if you want to minimize the harmful effects of training on your muscles. There are two simple methods. Calcium and magnesium each can reduce the secretion of parathyroid hormone, by distinct but complementary mechanisms.

It's not a matter of taking high doses for a brief period. Instead, you want to reinforce your intake of the two minerals in a moderate but continual way. I suggest taking magnesium and calcium separately if you supplement with tablets. Take the calcium one to two hours *before training*, which gives you an increased level of calcium in your blood at the time of training and should counteract the training-induced lowering of blood calcium. Although no one really knows how training increases PTH secretion, a reduced blood calcium level might be one of the stimulants.

Magnesium has some relaxing and tranquilizing effects, so you want to use it *at night* before you sleep. The dosages should depend on your nutritional intake and bodyweight. Bodybuilders who avoid dairy products need more calcium than others. A total daily supply of at least 2 grams is recommended.[1] For magnesium—and depending on the amount you get from food and protein drinks—500 milligrams to 1 gram of supplemental magnesium a day will produce visible results.[2] As studies have demonstrated, a magnesium supplement doesn't do much on its own.[3] It's the total intake of magnesium from food *and* supplements that really matters.

References

1. Klesges, R. C. 1996. Changes in bone mineral content in male athletes: Mechanisms of action and intervention effects. *JAMA.* 276:226.
2. Brilla, L. R. 1992. Effects of magnesium supplementation on strength training in humans. *J Am Coll Nutr.* 11:326.
3. Brilla, L. R. 1997. Effect of magnesium-fortified sports drink on strength in collegiate football players. *Med Sci Sports Exerc.* 29 (suppl):250.
4. Helbig, J. 1989. Vergleichende Untersuchungen zur Wirkung einer Magnesiumsubstitution bei Laufern und Kraftsportlern. *Magnesium Bull.* 11:34.
5. Rong, H. 1997. Effect of acute endurance and strength exercise on circulating calcium-regulating hormones and bone markers in young healthy males. *Scand J Med Sci Sports.* 7:152.

Lee Labrada.

Chapter 20

TOP 10 REASONS WHY ATHLETES SHOULD TAKE SUPPLEMENTS

BY DAVID PROKOP

No, you didn't tune in to the *Late Show with David Letterman* by mistake, and this topic is in no way funny if you're a serious athlete. However, with apologies to Mr. Letterman, we'll use the format he's popularized and illustrate why athletes should take—in fact, must take—nutritional supplements if they want to perform at their best. Many of these reasons are just plain common sense, but chances are you've never thought of the majority of them.

10. **Athletes can least afford to have nutritional deficiencies.** Since serious athletes place peak demands on their bodies in the pursuit of physical excellence, they can least afford to have nutritional deficiencies in their diet. Nutritional supplementation is a way to guard against such deficiencies.

9. **Our modern diet cannot guarantee you're getting all the nutrients in the amounts you need them.** We would like to think that our regular diet provides us with all the nutrients we need. But the truth is that the widespread use of pesticides and hormones in modern agriculture, not to mention the ways foods are processed, can seriously decrease the nutritional content of these foods. It is no surprise that more and more people today feel you're kidding yourself if you think you're getting all the nutrients you need, in the amounts you need them, from your regular diet. Such a nutritional shortfall can be a problem for even a sedentary person, but for an athlete pushing to the very limit in training and competition it can be downright disastrous.

8. **Athletes have a higher demand for the various nutrients than sedentary people do.** Not only is it true that the modern diet cannot guarantee you'll get all the nutrients you need, but athletes and others who exercise regularly need greater amounts of most nutrients due to the demands of their sport or activity. So, even if you were to assume that

Don Long.

your regular diet was providing enough nutrients to meet the recommended daily allowances (RDA), that may still not be enough. People who exercise a lot often need to exceed the RDA for the various nutrients—sometimes by a large margin.

7. **Supplementation is an excellent way to fine-tune your nutrition for your particular sport.** Different sports have different nutritional demands (e.g., bodybuilders need to consume above-average amounts of protein, and endurance athletes have a greater demand for carbohydrates). In many cases, athletes take supplements not simply for health reasons but because a higher-than-normal amount of the nutrient will enhance performance, whether that enhancement comes in the form of greater energy or endurance, a leaner body due to a greater thermo-genic (fat-burning) effect, greater mus-

cle mass from a higher testosterone level, or any of the myriad other benefits nutritional supplements can provide. Supplementation is an effective way to augment your intake of a particular nutrient when you want or need more than the amount of the nutrient your everyday diet provides.

6. **Many important substances simply are not part of a normal diet.** Even if you happened to be on a diet that was per-fection itself, some substances simply aren't part of a regular diet. Thus, the only way to get them is through supple-mentation. Since these supplements can have a variety of beneficial effects (e.g., boosting the immune system, increasing the body's fat-burning capacity, enhanc-ing the body's testosterone production), it can be said that if you want to combat illness, burn fat, or build muscle natu-rally, a ready answer is, of course, nutri-tional supplementation!

Aaron Baker.

5. **Supplementation is a way to get large amounts of a nutrient without needing to eat a lot of food (and calories) to get it.** In some instances getting sufficient or optimum amounts of a nutrient would require consuming so much food, and perhaps calories, that it would be prohibitive. Or, as one magazine recently put it: "The truth is, even the most balanced diets can't realistically provide optimal amounts of certain nutrients—unless you're willing to eat like a horse." Therefore, you're forced to rely on supplementation to get optimum amounts of such nutrients.

For example, to get enough pyruvate into your body to produce a significant effect, you'd have to eat eight red apples a day. Even Johnny Appleseed wouldn't want to eat that many apples. Here's perhaps an even more dramatic example of the same idea: you'd have to consume 8 cups of almonds or 62 cups of fresh spinach every day to get your RDA of vitamin E.

4. **Certain nutrients are best absorbed in supplement form.** According to some studies, it appears that nutrients like folic acid and vitamin K are easier for the body to use in supplement form than from actual food because these nutrients are more easily absorbed in pill form.

3. **Supplementation gives you a nutritional safety margin when you're on a weight-loss diet.** Athletes who need to reduce their bodyfat to a low percentage or to make a particular weight for their

Will Willis.

J. J. Marsh.

Katy Rickman.

sport often go on restricted-calorie diets. In the process they may unintentionally shortchange themselves in some key nutrients, which could affect performance. Supplementation is a way to safeguard against such nutritional deficiencies. By taking the nutrient in supplement form, you get the nutrient without the associated calories found in food.

2. **Supplementation is the athlete's psychological and physiological insurance policy regarding nutrition.** Even if you're very conscious of nutrition and are on a balanced, high-quality diet, there's no way to really know whether you're getting enough of the nutrients you need for peak performance. Short of going through a series of tests on a regular basis, you can assure yourself that everything is in order by simply taking nutritional supplements. This can have an important psychological effect on your athletic endeavors, even if it were to have no physiological effect. Simply knowing that you're doing everything possible in your training and for your nutrition to be at your best is, in and of itself, a significant psychological boost.

Henrik Thamasian's attitude is typical of many competitive athletes (or at least competitive bodybuilders) when he says, "I'd rather spend a dollar or two a day on vitamins, minerals, and other supplements even if they don't do me any good at all and I just eliminate them in my urine than run the risk of being deficient in some of the key nutrients."

And the number-one reason to take nutritional supplements if you're an athlete:

1. **Supplementation enables an athlete to perform better, period!** Even if you don't have nutritional deficiencies, you will perform better if you're on a performance supplementation program. The reason why should be obvious by now. Since performance is the bottom line in athletics, the fact that nutri-

tional supplementation will enhance performance, even if there are no nutritional deficiencies, is the clinching argument.

Leading sports nutritionist and former competitive bodybuilder Phil Goglia, director of Fitness Concepts in Venice, California, has worked with numerous athletes and celebrities on their nutrition. His clients have included Olympic champion sprinter Quincy Watts, champion bodybuilder Flex Wheeler, and the well-known actors Jeff Goldblum, Laura Dern, and Gillian Anderson. He says: "I don't think the entire medical community is ready to admit it, but from a performance standpoint the facts are clear. Recent history shows that if you take two athletes that have basically the same genetics, the same type of training, and the same type of diet, but one is taking nutritional supplementation for performance and the other one is not, you'll find that the one who's supplemented for performance will consistently exceed the other."

Katy Rickman.

INDEX